Changing Course

*Women's Inspiring
Stories of Menopause,
Midlife, and
Moving Forward*

Yitta Halberstam

Adams Media
Avon, Massachusetts

Published by
Adams Media, an F+W Publications Company
57 Littlefield Street, Avon, MA 02322. U.S.A.
www.adamsmedia.com

ISBN: 1-59337-091-1

Printed in Canada.

J I H G F E D C B A

Library of Congress Cataloging-in-Publication Data
Mandelbaum, Yitta Halberstam
Changing course / Yitta Halberstam.
p.   cm.
ISBN 1-59337-091-1
1. Middle aged women—Fiction. 2. Menopause—Fiction. I. Title.

PS3613.A535C48 2004
813'.6—dc22
2004009167

This publication is designed to provide accurate and authoritative information with
regard to the subject matter covered. It is sold with the understanding that the publisher is not engaged in rendering legal, accounting, or other professional advice. If legal
advice or other expert assistance is required, the services of a competent professional
person should be sought.
   —From a *Declaration of Principles* jointly adopted by a Committee of the American
            Bar Association and a Committee of Publishers and Associations

Many of the designations used by manufacturers and sellers to distinguish their
products are claimed as trademarks. Where those designations appear in this book
and Adams Media was aware of a trademark claim, the designations have been
printed with initial capital letters.

While all of the stories in this book are true, some of the names, dates, and places
have been changed to protect anonymity.

Interior photograph of shell © 2003 Brand X Pictures

This book is available at quantity discounts for bulk purchases.
For information, call 1-800-872-5627.

Dedication

For my husband, Motty, whose love, devotion, and inspiration
gives me the courage to change course, the patience to stay
on course, and the permission to sail away.

Permissions

Contents

Acknowledgments

As my *Small Miracles* series indicates, I don't believe in luck, chance, fate, or happenstance. So instead of saying "I'm so lucky," I'd rather say that I've been very blessed and fortunate to work with a coterie of bright, professional people who help make the writing and publishing process such a joy and adventure.

Gary M. Krebs, my brilliant and savvy editor, embodies an unusual combination of admirable attributes: He's exceptionally intelligent, creative, visionary, and organized! (Now that's unusual!) His passion for this book and enthusiasm were contagious and heartening, and it's simply great having him at the helm. Kate McBride, managing editor, had a special fondness for this particular project, and her vision and input significantly helped guide and shape its content and direction. Special thanks also to Gary's competent and gracious assistant Kirsten Amann for her assistance in many ways. Gene Molter, publicist extraordinaire, is a dynamo and an extraordinary professional to boot, and it has been fun and a joy to work with such a capable and conscientious individual. Richard Pine and Lori Entiman of Arthur Pine Associates are tops in their field, and it is a privilege to work with them. Thank you all!

This anthology was born out of a conversation I had with my good friend, Pessy Dinnerstein. I complained to her that I could not find inspiring and positive books about menopause to help me on my own personal journey, and she advised me to work on one myself. Conversations with Pessy always seem to bear exceptional fruit, and I am so grateful to her for being my friend. Thank you, Pessy.

I also want to thank another close and wonderful friend, Bella Friedman, who has come to my rescue more than once in my writing lifetime. Unlike my editor, Gary Krebs, I am not exactly the organized type, and Bella—a computer marvel—has oftentimes responded to my emergency calls when copy mysteriously vanishes from the computer screen, or when a virus has invaded the machine completely. She has patiently and kindly retyped hundreds of pages that were swallowed up in cyberspace and does preliminary readings of my various books as well. Beyond her technological miracles, Bella is a warm, supportive, and wonderful human being whose friendship I value tremendously. Thank you, Bella!

This book—and the previous seven books I have worked on—could never have been actualized had it not been for the assistance of an exceptional individual, Anna Ashton, who has been my right-hand woman for sixteen years. There is no way that I can ever repay Anna for all that she has done for me and given to me, and I cherish her friendship. One day I'll have to write a book about her, because in her own right she embodies the spirit and message of this book. (She's just a tad too young to qualify!) She, too, has changed course midstream and is now well on her way to becoming a full-fledged physician's assistant (PA). The medical community's assured gain will be my own personal loss, but I am happy for her and admire the tenacious way Anna has pursued her dreams and is now on the verge of attaining them. Thank you, Anna, for everything!

I am blessed with other wonderful people in my life—and I want to tell them how much they mean to me. Sara Laya Landa, Ruchama King Feuerman, Miriam Kalikstein, Etta Answel, Annette Grauman, Naomi Mauer, Sheila Abrams, Miriam Halberstam, Moishe and Evelyn Halberstam, Rabbi Leib and Sima Mandelbaum, Suri and Daniel Dymshitz, Chaim and Baila Mandelbaum, Yeruchem and Chaya Winkler: Thank you for your loving presence, your constant help and overall supportiveness. My colleagues at EMUNAH of America, in particular Carol Sufian and Melanie Oelbaum, are the most patient and understanding people in the world! My work habits here are erratic to say the least—mostly in part due to book tours, speeches, and writing commitments—but my colleagues kindly give me complete freedom to work at my own regular pace. I deeply value their support and friendship.

Noreen Harnik, proprietor of Harnik's bookstore in Brooklyn, has been the most generous and encouraging bookseller I have ever met. Together with her very personable, lovable, and talented assistant Rose, she has hand-sold thousands of *Small Miracles* books, the series I coauthored before this book. But much more than this, Noreen and Rose are warm and loving friends, enthusiastic champions, and exceptional individuals whom it is a pleasure and privilege to know. Many thanks to Minnie and Evan of Harnik's, too!

The best part about writing *Small Miracles* has been the sweet and strong friendship I have developed with my coauthor, Judith Leventhal, whom I treasure so much. Her intelligence, zany sense of humor, and deep psychological insights have enriched my life. Raizy Steg has been the most wonderful, loving, and generous friend I could ever imagine anyone being blessed with, and I am truly thankful to God for her presence in my life.

Georgie Klein, whose amazing creativity inspires awe and admiration, is always there for me—day and night. Thank you, Georgie!

Carolyn Hessel is the best champion, cheerleader, and friend any writer could ever hope for. The executive director of the national Jewish Book Council, she took me under her wing when I was an unknown author, believed in me, and helped make *Small Miracles* a household name. She is one of the most generous, caring, and professional people I know, and I want to thank her for the tremendous impact she has had on my life and work. Thank you, Carolyn!

Like the Academy Award presentations, I leave the best for the last! Motty, my husband, and my children, Yossi and Eli Mandelbaum: You are my lights, my joys, my treasures. You give the deepest meaning and value to my life. And without your love, generosity, and support, I could never have been able to produce eight books. What a blessing to have you all in my life.

My parents of blessed memory—Rabbi Laizer Halberstam and Claire Halberstam—are no longer alive, but they are still very much with me. Their spirit and their legacy informs this—indeed, *every*—book I have worked on, every newspaper and magazine article, every story, every poem. I hope that somehow they know how much love I feel toward them, how grateful I am for everything they gave me, and how much I wish they were here to enjoy the fruits of their labor.

And above all, I want to thank God. There are hundreds of thousands of talented writers out in the world, and few are ever afforded the exceptional opportunities that I have been blessed with. I know that God is at the heart of this blessing, and I feel privileged to be in a position that so many others richly deserve. I pray to be able to produce only positive books that uplift people and encourage them, and with this work, I hope I am indeed fulfilling my mission.

~ Yitta Halberstam

No one grows old by living,
only by losing interest in living.

~ Marie Beynon Ray

Introduction

In December 2002, I skipped my period for the first time in my life (barring pregnancies, of course). I wasn't duly concerned. I had done a lot of traveling during my book tour in November and assumed that crisscrossing the United States on twenty-five flights in the span of one month had been at least partially responsible for disrupting my cycle. Still, when several weeks passed, and menstruation didn't return, I bought my first home pregnancy test. Then I bought a second, and a few days later returned home from the pharmacy with a third. Within the next three weeks, I took a total of eight home pregnancy tests, all of which were negative. "I don't know what's wrong with these home pregnancy tests," I fretted indignantly to my husband. "No matter which brand I buy, each one is defective. That's it: I'm going to the doctor tomorrow morning to get a blood test from a reliable lab." My husband rolled his eyes.

I thought the doctor looked as if he were about to choke on something when I hurtled into his office the next day and demanded a pregnancy test, but I was so deep in the throes of my obsession to finally know the truth (that yes, I was indeed pregnant) that I failed to fully register the strange look that appeared on his face or the chortle that erupted from his room when I exited. I was too busy thinking about baby clothes and Lamaze classes to note the strained look of incredulity that appeared fleetingly on his face and which he valiantly tried to squash, quickly recomposing his features into a mask of utter seriousness.

A few days later, my husband casually inquired, "So, did you get the results of the pregnancy test yet?"

"Don't you think the doctor would have called me if it was positive?" I asked, surprised.

"Call *you*?" my husband snorted rudely. "He wouldn't call *you*. He'd call the media!"

You wouldn't think that it would take all this time for the truth to dawn upon a fairly intelligent, well-read human being (meaning me), but denial can seize anybody in its fog-induced haze. It only took a total of nine pregnancy tests, my husband's acerbic wit, and my doctor's discomfiture for me to finally make the connection between the sudden cessation of my menses, my age, and reality. *Ohmygod,* I gasped in horror, *it's menopause!*

As a typical, proactive baby-boomer, I switched into whirl-wind mode and in quick succession made a foray to the local Barnes & Noble to hunt for books on menopause, conferred with friends who had already graduated to "wise women" status, and scheduled an appointment with an idealistic nutri-tionist who helps women on the cusp of menopause. No sooner had I handed over a hefty $500 fee (alas, the nutritionist wasn't as idealistic as originally reported) to her for my first consultation that I discovered that I was the butt of a cosmic joke. Almost as soon as I left the nutritionist's office, a small, familiar twinge in the pit of my stomach heralded the ironic but welcome news that my period had finally arrived and $500 poorer, I rushed to the pharmacy to buy a fresh supply of

Tampax. Indeed, it had been the excessive air travel after all that had disrupted my menstrual cycle, and my self-proclaimed trajectory to "crone" had been excessively premature.

Thrilled though I was to return to my former exalted position of Tampax and Advil consumer, this brief episode had enormous reverberations for me, both as a woman and as an author. For, during the course of this short-lived interlude, I had stumbled upon some astonishing facts.

First, as a typical baby-boomer, I had instantly rushed to the local bookstore to educate myself about menopause (a subject I had not been galvanized to study previously) and was startled to discover that most books about this subject were shelved in the "Disease" section of the store (I promise!). Secondly, almost all of the books I found were about the nutritional, medical, health, and hormonal aspects of menopause, with only a handful devoted to the psychological and spiritual issues that accompany the physical changes of menopause. Thirdly, the few books that I did find about the "menopausal/ midlife journey" written from an emotional perspective were mostly first-person accounts by celebrities who do not have to grapple with many of the ordinary difficulties of day-to-day life that besiege us lesser mortals and whose experiences therefore were mostly irrelevant to me.

I did finally stumble upon a self-published anthology that seemed, at initial glance, to offer the symphony of varied voices that I was seeking, but upon reading it, I discovered that the perspectives were uniformly negative, and I ended up feeling far more depressed than I had been at the start.

Over the past five years, since I began touring for the six *Small Miracles* books I coauthored, I have been tremendously gratified to hear one common phrase repeated to me by effusive women from all over the United States: "Your books make me feel so good. They banish the blues. You can't imagine what they've done for me. Thank you for making me feel there's a hope." It was only after I surveyed the sample of literature that exists on menopause and midlife, that I suddenly had the epiphany, the *a-ha!* moment. "I know what I'm looking for," I realized in mounting excitement. "I'm looking for a *Small Miracles*–type book about midlife and menopause . . . a book containing many voices that is positive, upbeat, encouraging, and feel-good. Not Pollyanna-ish, not saccharine-sweet, but nonetheless a collection of stories that dwells on the upside of midlife and imparts the message that midlife can be a new chapter, one that offers opportunities for growth, change, increased creativity, new careers, new loves, new hobbies, and so on. There just has to be a book like this around." But when I could not find one that fulfilled my criteria—despite persistent hunting both in bookstores and on the Internet alike—the concept for *Changing Course: Women's Inspiring Stories of Menopause, Midlife, and Moving Forward* was born.

Changing Course is an upbeat anthology geared to women who are about to enter menopause, are experiencing it now, or who have just exited it and are wondering "What's next?" The book contains stories and essays by diverse "ordinary" women who come from all spectrums and streams of life and who view menopause and midlife from a positive perspective. Their stories emphasize that midlife is a new door to something else: a second adulthood, a different chapter, a time for growth, change, and new opportunities, and that it need not be viewed with fear, dread, or despair.

"The signal of midlife," says therapist Jane Einhorn, "is the moment you think, not how old am I, but how much time do I have left?" Facing mortality adds special urgency and poignancy to reclaiming abandoned dreams, revisiting old passions, reinventing one's self. Contrary to the abundant myths stating that women in midlife are on a downward spiral toward decline, many women in the second half of their lives in fact awaken to drives, longings, and new awareness. Consequently, they return to school; start new businesses; recover old passions, hobbies, interests, and art forms; travel; pursue politics; and speak out. Margaret Mead called this phase "postmenopausal zest," a name that up until now remained a notion for discussion in professional circles only. Now that the baby-boom generation is unfolding the secret for the masses to embrace, *Changing Course* both describes and validates a different kind of approach to menopause and midlife. As George Eliot, the author, once said: "It is never too late to be what you might have been."

Changing Course contains stories and essays on a plethora of topics related to midlife and menopause, including midlife romances, adventures, reclaiming dreams, overcoming obstacles, confronting unfinished business of the past, parenting, speaking the truth, spirituality, aging, changing body appearances, taking better care of our bodies, caretaking older parents, friendships, the experience of menopause, returning to school, changing careers, relocation, and practically any other subject that falls within the purview of a midlife/menopausal experience, challenge, or triumph. Together, these stories form a narrative arc that testifies to the wisdom of Sophia Loren, who once said, "There *is* a fountain of youth. It is your mind, your talents, the creativity you bring to your life, and the lives of the people you love. When you learn to tap this source, you will truly have defeated age."

Working on this book and communicating with wise, powerful, and proactive women from all over the world has been an enormous blessing and adventure. With this anthology, I now turn this gift over to you, dear reader, and hope that you will gain as much insight and inspiration from their stories as I have. The personal accounts that form and shape this book have convinced me more than ever that middle age is the *center* of life, not the end of it, and that the best is yet to come. Age is an attitude, not a number, and rebirth and renewal can be ours at any time.

~ *Yitta Halberstam*

one

———◄o►———

Don't Look Back

I love my past.
I love my present.
I'm not ashamed of what I've had,
and I'm not sad because I have it no longer.

~ Colette

At the Container Store

by Joyce Maynard

I was moving, but not very far. The bright, big, and enormously cluttered house just north of San Francisco where I had lived for seven years with my children (first three of them, then two, then one, then none) had gotten too big for me, and definitely too expensive. My new home had to be smaller, more efficient, and cheaper to maintain.

I've always been the nesting type. Back when I was young and starting out my married life (and then parenthood), I baked my own bread and grew my own tomatoes for spaghetti sauce. The picture I held of midlife (as much as a woman in her twenties thinks about those things at all, which is not much) featured hearth and home—a garden, a pantry full of china, an art studio for projects, and lots of room for entertaining friends. Among my images of my future, one I never contemplated was that I would be living on my own, my children far from home, and myself too busy to grow vegetables, or that I'd be contemplating the prospect of selling my home to face the growing demands of college tuitions and savings wiped out in the stock market.

Twice before, I'd gone through the wrenching process of leaving a beloved home and clearing out all our possessions, and the thought of doing that again filled me with sadness and dread. So I cooked up an alternate plan: Rent out the main house. And move downstairs.

With the proceeds from a home equity loan, I made an apartment out of our formerly dirt-floor basement: living room, sleeping area, kitchenette, and bath. Because our home sits on the side of a mountain, the effect was not of living belowground but rather of being perched in the neat, tight cabin of a ship, with a good-sized deck extending beyond the door to my new place, looking out to the same spectacular view of the mountain and the San Francisco Bay. But if the horizon outside remained vast, the interior of my space definitely was not. And so came the problem: what to do with all of our stuff?

My new neighbor, Kate, was just in the process of moving in next door as I was shifting my own messy life from upstairs to down. Stopping by her newly set-up space one afternoon, after probably my thirty-fourth trip up and down stairs with boxes, I had felt a wave of calm and envy at the simplicity of how she'd set things up for herself. In the center of the living room was a grass mat, with a statue of the Buddha and a little altar to one side, holding a single crystal, a feather, and a bowl with three lemons in it. Nothing else.

But as much as I loved Kate's spare, peaceful haven, I couldn't emulate it. When I moved our things out of the house to prepare for the arrival of my tenants, I had set on the deck every worldly possession I owned, and everything belonging to my children, in one giant tumble. For days—as the scent of Kate's incense wafted over on the breeze—I sifted through belongings: old toys, school papers, my favorite dress from the seventies, an ancient Victrola and piles of 78s, my fifteen china teapots, my books, CDs, my salt-and-pepper-shaker collection, and piles of fabric from clothes no longer in my wardrobe that might be useful for some art project someday.

It was not surprising—given my sentimental feelings about the artifacts of our family's past—that even after I'd thinned out the items destined for a future yard sale and given away the dresses with padded shoulders and half of my cowboy boots, I was still left with a huge and daunting mountain of possessions.

Rather than divest myself of everything, I chose the option of storage. I may not want to make waffles this week, or this year, but the day will come, and when it does, what if I've parted with my waffle iron? I may not have an occasion coming up that calls for a beaded evening gown—but who knows when I might be nominated for an Oscar?

A new store had opened near me a few months earlier whose specialty was beautiful, high-efficiency storage containers. I had pored over their catalog. I spent a morning measuring the spaces I had to work with. Now I drove over to make my purchases.

If Kate's home had spoken of one kind of beautiful, minimalist order, the vast aisles of the Container Store suggested another, somewhat more attainable for a person like me. It may be avoidance to take the baggage of your life and—rather than making a clean break with it—stick the stuff in boxes. But I decided that, for myself at least, there is only so much letting go a person can do at once.

Once at the Container Store, I maneuvered my cart through the aisles more slowly than usual, not simply taking in the containers on the shelves, but imagining the pieces of my life I could put in them. In Aisle Four were boxes for photographs.

Eight had CD shelving. Six, sealed plastic boxes perfect for my vintage ski sweaters and kimono collection. Along the back wall, shelving components, mix and match.

The last fifteen years had featured plenty of upheaval in my life: the death of my mother, a long and bitter divorce, a cross-country move with my children, and, in recent years, the wrenching process of watching them take off, one by one, for their own big and necessary adventures. I had lived through more than a couple of relationships—and seen their endings—before finally forming the one I tell my children and friends will actually last.

Through it all, I had continued to seek a sense of order amid the physical and emotional clutter. Now, among the Rubbermaid containers and lidded bamboo boxes and brightly colored storage crates, I allowed myself to believe I might actually be ready to attain it.

It was a slow day at the Container Store. The woman at the cash register, when I came to check out, seemed in no hurry. So we chatted.

"Moving?" she asked. Sort of, I told her, and then explained.

Barbara looked to be about my age—poking fifty with a short stick. I guessed, from her nod of recognition, that she might be divorced, like me, with the last child gone from home or nearing that point.

"Freshman, UC Santa Barbara," she said of her daughter. "Now I'm wondering what to do with my life. I feel like I could go anyplace, as long as it doesn't cost an arm and a leg."

Another woman had joined in our conversation now, too. "I wish I could move into my basement," she said. "I love my house, but I'd love my freedom more. I worry about making the mortgage payment every month. And what's the point of a big house, with nobody in it anymore?"

Out in the parking lot, I loaded my containers in the trunk of my convertible and headed for home. I spent the rest of the day sorting fragments of my life—tax returns, jewelry, the clip from my daughter's umbilical cord—into the appropriate containers and labeling them. By sunset, the mountain of stuff on my deck was noticeably smaller, though far from gone. The next morning at ten on the dot, I was back at the Container Store to buy more containers. Barbara was back at her post.

"I hoped we hadn't seen the last of you," she said.

It took forty-nine years, collecting all this stuff, I told her. It would take more than forty-eight hours, putting it away.

She had been thinking about the plan I'd set up, she told me. She didn't want to sell her house either. Maybe, with a nice little studio in the basement, and the right containers, she wouldn't have to.

A coworker of Barbara's named Larry approached us. "Studio in the basement?" he said. "Cool." Larry was way too young to be an empty nester (probably hadn't even made his nest yet). Still, he liked the idea of what I was doing.

"I wish my mom would do something like that," he said. "She keeps our house just like it was in high school, like it's Graceland or something. It's a little depressing going back to visit."

I had worried, actually, that my own three kids might feel displaced by my decision to dismantle our home and downsize so radically. "Let me tell you something," said Larry. "What you want from your mom, at a stage like this, is just knowing that she's happy and not stressed out. You want her to get on with her own life, so she won't be on your case all the time."

Barbara was ringing up my new assortment of containers, meanwhile, and making suggestions (based on what I had picked out) of other items I could find helpful, that might have escaped my notice. Knowing I was a writer, maybe I'd like a few of their manuscript boxes? Cedar chips, to get rid of that telltale basement aroma?

Our friend from the day before was nowhere to be seen, but Barbara and I were bonded like old friends now. "I was thinking about you last night," she said. "I see a lot of women at our stage of life, coming into the store. People whose kids have left home. People who have lost jobs, who have to move. There's a lot of stories in a place like this."

She told me about a trip she'd made recently to San Miguel in Mexico. She had thought about moving there. I told her about the little village on the shores of a mountain lake in Guatemala, where I bought a house cheap enough I could pay cash. I go there for a few weeks or a few months at a time, but if I ever lose everything, I can always go there, I told her.

"This isn't how we thought we were going to be living our lives when we got to this age, is it?" said a woman (yet another new friend from the checkout line). "I always figured I'd be married, doing bargello or something, by this stage. Not taking off in a Winnebago with no forwarding address."

"A friend of mine got an old houseboat," someone said. "She put everything she owned in watertight plastic tubs and—off she went."

"It's all about the containers," Barbara's coworker Larry offered. "There's a container for everything."

Driving home, after settling up my bill (organizing your life does not come cheap), I thought about that line. Hauling my boxes down the steps along the side of my house past

Kate's altar and hot tub to the nearly tidy deck out in front of my apartment, I considered all the times in the last fifteen years I've hauled possessions from one place to another, thrown possessions into plastic trash bags or liquor store boxes, and piled them in the back seat of my car. I thought about divorce interrogatories and tax returns, financial aid forms, mortgage applications, letters from old boyfriends, wedding pictures from a marriage long dissolved. I had spent a few hundred dollars on containers, over the course of my three days' worth of trips to the Container Store. If the result yielded an ability to truly pack away the past in such a manner that it wouldn't clutter up the present and the future, the stuff was a bargain.

I had chosen sage green to store my book manuscripts, blue plastic baskets for my skin-care products, and a zippered purple pouch to put my mother's ashes in until I can make the trip to Mexico—a place she loved and visited annually in her own post-childraising, post-divorce days—to scatter them. Thanks to the boxes—neatly labeled and stacked in the crawl space where I'll know they're there without having to see them every day—I managed to make for myself a space that is neat, orderly, and tranquil. A home nice enough, ironically, that leaving will be easy. (This month, for instance, I am staying with my partner on an island in British Columbia. Come winter, I'll be drawn to Guatemala.)

Later that afternoon, I invited my neighbor Kate to stop by for tea, brewed in one of my fifteen teapots and poured into two of the thirty-two bone china cup-and-saucer sets from my grandmother I didn't have the heart to put into the yard sale box; they were neatly arranged on my new modular shelving now. If my new friend Barbara hadn't been working, I would have invited her to stop by, too, to celebrate. But I had a feeling I'd be seeing her again, one way or another.

"Good job," said Kate. "You really put your life in order."

Over our heads, we could hear the faint, sweet sound of small feet—my new tenants' children. The sound was oddly comforting, like a gentle summer rain. I took a sip of tea.

"This will be a nice place for your grandchildren to visit, when you have some," Kate said, studying the bin marked "Cake toppers," and the one on the shelf next to it. "Glitter, sequins, and miscellaneous jewels," read the label. Because a person still needs to hold on to her jewels sometimes. She may simply wish to contain them. ❧

The Baby, the Bathwater, and the Bathtub

by Carol L. Skolnick

*I*t took me close to twenty years, but when I turned forty-four I got a clue. Within a few months' time, I had given away nearly all of the hundreds of children's books I'd collected during the years I worked in educational publishing. I was keeping them for the baby I believed I'd have one day. It finally dawned on me that this day was not likely to come.

My desire to be a mother was always at war with the reality I have lived. I've never married, never even came close to it. I used to chalk it up to being unlucky in love. More recently, I have come to see things differently, to understand how I've played it safe all my life, out of the desire to spare any future child of mine the kind of pain I went through—the pain of living in an unstable home with parents who did not love each other; the pain of being inadequately cared for by a depressed mother who could barely take care of herself. Because I loved the idea of my as-yet unborn children more than I loved myself, I was waiting for the exact perfect conditions for their arrival: a good husband-father candidate, financial stability, my own emotional availability. At no time in my life have all three of these factors been present at once.

At forty-four, with a changing body and diminishing returns on my psychological and financial investments, I realized I was living in uncontrolled clutter. The cause of that clutter was about clinging, not to new life, but to recent death. The stuff I have kept is symbolic of that which is no longer alive in me: the saris, deity statues, and other accoutrements of eight years' participation in an Eastern religious sect; accessories like silver candlesticks and highball glasses, bought for the Barbie Dream House my late mother tried to build and that I would never live in; clothes three sizes too small and many years out of date; files from a dying business that I can't seem to resurrect; and the precious, timeless tales I hoped to share with a tiny girl or boy who would look like me, look up to me, and love me.

Beyond biological urges, why are we compelled to reproduce? My reasons were partly societal. As a middle-class, heterosexually inclined American woman, I never dreamed I wouldn't. But there was something else, I think—the impulse to reparent myself in the form of another. When the utter hopelessness of this agenda came to the fore, it coincided with the unlikelihood of its happening in the usual way, given my age and marital status, my money struggles, my recurrent descents into despondency. I'd made my choice years ago, many times, each time I left a relationship. If I'd truly wanted a baby above all other things, I would have struggled on that path alone or with a man I did not love, toughed it out in a regular job with baby benefits and biweekly paychecks.

Coming to terms with childlessness has not been easy. I love children, but at the same time they have always made me weep. It is excruciating to accompany my friends and their little ones to the playground, where mommies and nannies congregate while toddlers play, where everything I never had and won't have is so very present. And yet, in mentally throwing away not only the baby's bathwater but also the baby and even the bathtub, I finally feel okay to take care of myself, to mother me. I do that in small but significant ways, when I eat well, when I exercise regularly, when I tell myself I've done a good job, when I take a bubble bath, whenever I resist the urge to beat myself up for making a mistake. No one ever made a baby book for me, so I have done that, collecting crumbling Polaroids and school pictures, snapshots from my junior year abroad and my fortieth birthday party—putting them all in an album so that I may delight in my own growth from six days old to now. A little child of forty-four deserves that much.

It also occurs to me, as I hand each little picture book over to my delighted young friends and relatives, that I can have no real regrets because I have lived my integrity. I did what I said I would do. No children were harmed in the making of this picture. I have loved and protected my unborn as I could not have done had they taken birth. They have been spared; and so, perhaps, have I.

My Mother's Menopause

by Yitta Halberstam

ow perverse it is that it is often only with distance and time that insights become sharpened and more astute, powers of observation heightened and enhanced. We need to grasp the nature of things and people in the *present,* in the *now,* but often that is precisely when they elude us, or when we delude ourselves. So often clarity comes too late, when it can no longer be put in service of the living.

I think of misperceptions and misconceptions today, as I simultaneously prepare to both celebrate the publication of this book and to commemorate the second anniversary of my mother's death. Working on *Changing Course* has given me cause for both reverie and reflection. I think about the women I know for whom midlife has been a transition to something better—a new door to something else, a bridge to a more authentic self. I surprise myself with an epiphany when I decide that of all the role models I know, none embodies this concept better than my own mother, Claire Halberstam.

It's a new awareness, never fully realized before—an understanding that barely skittered on the fringes of my mind. Perhaps I was too close to see her; it is, after all, only when we step back and look from a distance that an entire picture comes into view. And what a delicious find, such an unexpected treasure! To suddenly realize that out of all the women I know, my mother best embodies the concept that is both the mandate and mission of this book. Like unheard whispers or gossamer threads, the Truth was there all the time, waiting to be mined. And no one could be more stunned by this revelation than my very own self.

My mother was a shy, retiring housewife. Or at least that's what she was until she turned forty-five. She did all the requisite things housewives born out of the complacent, pre-feminist 1950s did: She cooked, she baked, she sewed, she kept house. I never thought of her as a dynamo. It was always my charismatic journalist/writer father who took center stage in our home and community. My mother was like all my friends' mothers—well-bred, reserved, silent. I did not know that she felt stifled and that she yearned for a voice of her own.

But one day—it seemed like it happened overnight—a dramatic shift began taking place in my mother: Suddenly she transformed into a butterfly of the most magnificent colors. My siblings and I looked at her not in admiration but with incredulity and, I am sorry to say, something akin to pity and disdain. After all, we were teenagers and young adults, in the throes of our power, and from our puerile vantage point, my mother seemed to be at the cusp of old age. How could she reinvent herself at the ripe old age of . . . oh my goodness . . . forty-five?

But reinvent herself she did, with dogged determination—almost fury. She began taking classes in Manhattan almost every evening, classes in alternative healing, positive thinking, Silva mind control, yoga meditation, macrobiotics—anything and everything off the beaten track beckoned her. We siblings watched with astonishment as our mother raced to classes in topics that were esoteric and on the cutting edge of twentieth-century thought, as she brought home tote bags stuffed with catalogs from schools we had never heard of and subjects we didn't even know existed. She pored over the catalogs end-lessly and enrolled in an endless number of classes. She studied with a host of teachers and then became a teacher herself. We were numb with shock when she announced she had become a teacher of meditation at a Manhattan Y; we blinked when she told us that she was going to bring these ideas to her com-munity and create an "Alternative Healing Center" in the heart of Brooklyn—from within the very heart of our home. How long, we wondered, would this phase go on? (It would go on for the rest of her lifetime, until her death at the young age of seventy-two.)

Suddenly, our mother—this shy, retiring housewife—had metamorphosed into a veritable dynamo herself. We hadn't known how her voice had been muffled all these years and how much she longed to speak. We told her that Brooklyn was not yet ready for "alternative healing," but undeterred by our discouragement, she established the Alternative Healing Center anyway. The Alternative Healing Center brought the then-revolutionary concept of healthy eating, nutrition, and macro-biotics to a relatively unsophisticated neighborhood, creating important inroads in people's consciousness—indeed, in their lives. Every Sunday night, the Center featured a macrobiotic buffet, prepared by a macrobiotic chef who had studied at and was certified by the world-famous Kushi Institute. Several weekdays at night, the Center offered classes in a variety of esoteric topics, ranging from healing with magnets to color therapy to shiatsu. Practitioners who were renowned in their respective fields trekked down to the wilds of Brooklyn to deliver lectures and seminars and, when they arrived, they searched for the offices of the staff administering this popular facility. There was no staff—my mother initiated and implemented everything by herself—and the facility in which all the lectures took place was the upstairs of my parents' home. People marveled that one woman could pull all of this together by herself.

After my mother died, the testimonials started to pour in. *"Your mother changed my life"*; *"I became macrobiotic because of her"*; *"She introduced me to a whole new way of looking at things"*; *"I met my husband at your mother's event"* (oh, yes, she also "did" Jewish singles events and parties); *"She was an amazing woman. She set her mind on something, and her will was so strong, she never stopped until she got what she wanted."*

So now, as I begin to prepare for two momentous milestones in my life—the publication of this book and the commemoration of my mother's second *yarhrzeit* (anniversary of her death), I think about my mother and how we did not have an easy personal relationship, which made it difficult for me to see her with clarity. But now that almost two years have passed, I realize poignantly all the things I never realized before . . .

If anyone ever epitomized the concept that midlife can become a new point of embarkation and that personal growth is never subject to age, it was my mother. Because of her, I fear not the specter of diminished abilities or curtailed activities but, rather, welcome the freedom that comes with being "a woman of a certain age"—a wise woman. Because of her,

I fear not the specter of failure but the fear of never trying, for that is the greatest failure of all.

How little I appreciated her courage and the strength of her convictions while she lived. It is ironic I only truly see her now that she is gone. I vow that her lesson—her legacy—will not be lost, and for as long as I possibly can, I will dance. ✄

Finding Joy in Midlife

by Renie Burghardt

"You've never been alone, and you'll never make it on your own," my husband growled menacingly, as he was leaving the house with some of his things.

After many miserable years of marriage, I had finally gotten enough courage to file for divorce, but his words came back to haunt me that first year alone. It was true about never having been on my own. When I was married in the late fifties, I went from living at home with my gentle grandparents, who raised me, to living with a husband, who turned out to be a tyrant! It soon became obvious that nothing I did would ever please him, but I learned to live with it. After all, soon there were three kids to consider, along with a nice new house in the suburbs and winter vacations in Florida, so what did it matter that my self-esteem had hit rock bottom?

When the youth of old age, fifty, was looming on the horizon, and my kids were grown and living lives of their own, and my life had become nothing more than a series of panic attacks because of constant verbal abuse, I decided one day that enough was enough and filed for that divorce.

Of course, he had been right. Being alone was not something I was prepared for. Neither was working for a living. The divorce settlement included a house and a small income, but it wasn't enough of an income to cover the expenses of suburban living. Luckily, I was hired for the first job I applied for. It was a job at a Car Parts warehouse, so it wasn't anything to brag about, but it would help pay some of the bills and it was close to home.

So the first year alone was miserable. Whenever I was home from work, the television was blaring in the living room while the radio was doing the same in the kitchen. Not that I was watching or listening to either. They were on to fill the vacuum of silence, to give the illusion of someone being there with me.

That first Christmas, my two sons, who were in the armed services, came home on leave, and my newly married daughter and son-in-law were with me. But on New Year's Eve, I was alone and thought I'd die of loneliness. I remember how sorry I felt for myself as I sat in front of the television and thought about all the lucky people celebrating with friends and loved ones. I wanted to be out dancing and laughing and having fun, not crying myself to sleep long before the clock struck midnight!

Then spring arrived, and nature beckoned. I had always loved nature, and as a teenager used to submerge myself in books about her, vowing that one day, I would live in the country and enjoy her beauties to my heart's content. But for the time being, I decided, I could drive to the nearby Metro Park and fill my soul with the beauties of spring.

So there I was, driving through the park on a sunny day in early May. I parked, and walked to the clearing, sitting down on a picnic bench under a huge pine. There were several people there having a grand time. People with their dogs! There were black dogs chasing Frisbees, a yellow dog chasing a tennis ball, a wiener dog watching them, with his tail wagging—all kinds of people and dogs having fun together. And, as I sat there watching them, it suddenly dawned on me that I didn't have to be alone. I could get a dog of my own! My ex-spouse didn't approve of pets, but I loved animals and always had several pets as a child.

The following Monday, I visited our Humane Society. A short time later, I was driving home with a young black Lab, whose soulful eyes and wagging tail promised many happy days ahead. And in the cat carrier the Humane Society had lent me, two tabby scaredy-cats were about to get a new home, too. Suddenly, there was a black dog to romp with when I got home from work, and two cats to snuggle with, and life wasn't so bad after all.

Greatly encouraged now, I decided to visit my nearest public library next. It had been a favorite haunt in the past, but I had not been there in years. I felt like Alice in Wonderland! Browsing happily among the aisles of books, I was drawn to the books about nature and country living. I picked out several and settled in for a week of evening reading.

Gradually, it dawned on me that it wasn't enough just to read about nature and country living, I wanted to *be* in the country. And the vow I made to myself as a teenager surfaced and I decided it was now or never. I mean, I was alone, and there was no one to stop me from following my dream.

The next several months were filled with the excitement of searching for my special little country haven. By August of 1983, I had sold my house, and had a rustic house on 100 acres in a beautiful hill country. Some friends, those who couldn't believe I would just leave, tried to change my mind. But my kids were happy that I was going after my dream, and Sammy was looking forward to being a country dog!

In retrospect, I realize that I jumped into the decision without too much thought. But had I thought about it more, I may not have done it. I did have a small income to rely on, and although some of the money from the sale of my suburban property went to pay for my country place, there was also some money left over for emergencies. And I hoped to make some extra money from writing, that elusive dream I had never had time for in the city.

Now I live in a house in the woods. My most immediate neighbors are deer, raccoon, opossum, wild turkey, coyote, black bear, armadillos, snakes, and more, and I revere all of them.

Of course, there are dogs and cats, fluffy bantam chickens, and ducks adding their quacking to the special country ambiance. Who says "alone" has to be empty and miserable? Not I, that's for sure! I've been alone for several years now, and I have never felt happier and fuller.

I am so glad I had the fortitude to change my life. The old adage says, "Life is what you make it." I chose to find joy in midlife, and I've never been happier. 🐾

Baby Blues

by Betty Rollin

I am one of those old-time "career girls" who forgot to have children. Well, I didn't really forget. I was just busy. And ambitious. And because I was busy and ambitious (and okay, maybe a tad neurotic), I didn't marry until I was thirty-six. It was the start of the '70s, and the women's movement was just taking hold. It certainly had taken hold of me. I even wrote an in-your-face piece (for *Look* magazine) dumping on motherhood. Who needs it, I actually said: "The notion that the maternal wish and the activity of mothering are instinctive or biologically predestined is baloney." I didn't stop there. "A lot of evidence suggests that for more women than anyone wants to admit, motherhood can be miserable," I wrote. To explain why any woman in her right mind would want to enter such a state, I went on to talk about all the societal pressures to be a mother, not to mention the instant identity conferred by motherhood: "First, through wifehood, you are somebody's wife; then you are somebody's mother."

I remember writing that piece. It was the summer of 1970, and I had my research sprawled all over the dining room table in a big, old beach house I was sharing with Betty Friedan and a few other feminists and male sympathizers, one of whom was to become my first husband. I want to be fair to myself. The piece had some merit. I wrote about women who became mothers automatically, who perhaps shouldn't have; about the fact that there is a lot more to being a good mother than many women understood before they got pregnant. I talked about unhappy mothers who couldn't admit it. (Their rage was palpable in the mail I got.) And, I said, if you found motherhood didn't suit you, unlike marriage, you couldn't—and still can't—divorce your child. All good points. My problem was I took every word I wrote to heart. In those days, you lived what you wrote.

So no children for me. It wasn't a difficult choice. That first marriage lasted about five minutes, and even though I hooked up with a new boyfriend—who wanted children—I got breast cancer, and the oncologist said I'd better not. (Nowadays, that advice has changed. Lots of women who have had breast cancer go ahead and give birth with no ill effect.) The new boyfriend thought better of marrying a woman who couldn't have children—and my second husband, a mathematician, is the kind of tenderhearted person who is naturally sweet with children, but he told me he was happy not to own any. I think he realized that with children, noise and interruptions—two things he hated—would be part of the package. Anyway, by then we were both forty-two.

So fine. My career went roaring ahead. I went from magazine work to television. My books were made into television movies. I was riding high. I adored my husband—still do. We had great friends. I got better at cooking, and we turned out some terrific dinner parties. All was well. I had a second bout with breast cancer, but when that passed I felt the way I did the first time: lucky.

In my late forties, I noticed our friends' children were growing up into people. Some of them were really nice people, not to mention smart and attractive. Hmmm, I found this interesting, but in no way did this fact reach the internal me. By my fifties, the grandchildren began to appear. The photos looked alike to me, but I didn't say that. Then my mother died, and I was forced to notice that, except for my husband, I had no immediate family—no parents, no siblings, no children. I reconnected with a couple of cousins. I forged a new relationship with a nephew, my husband's brother's son who had moved to New York. I observed myself doing this, but in a detached way, with no emotion I was aware of.

Then I hit sixty. We thought, let's go to China before it's too late. In China, like everyone, I took photos. But I found myself not taking the photos that everyone else was taking. My photos were of people, but not just any people; they were of mothers and children. Mostly I clicked when a certain look happened between the mother and the child. To this day, I have one of those framed on a bookshelf in my living room. A woman sits on a stone step on an ancient, remote road. Her child, a chubby one-and-a-half- or two-year-old in light-blue overalls, stands sulkily on the step below. The mother is leaning back a bit, as if to get a full view of her little prince. The language of her look is clear: Look at him! Have you ever seen such an adorable boy?

I snapped, and something odd happened to me that had been happening throughout the trip. My eyes filled up. It wasn't that I was moved in that way one is moved at the sight of something apart from oneself. I was moved by the sight, yes, but the tears came from a stab I felt in my heart. I had no small creature of my own I could look at like that. I felt jealous. And jealousy turned rapidly into grief. My decision—even though it hadn't been totally my decision—had finally caught up with me. Right there in the remotest corner of western China, at the age of sixty, when of course if there were such a child in my life, he would be a grandchild, I began to mourn for the children I never had. I didn't talk about it to my husband. What was the point? We were traveling, and surely this would pass.

But when we got home it didn't pass. I saw mothers and their children everywhere, all with that look. On the street, on the bus, in airports, in supermarkets. I learned to look away. When our friends talked about their children (which some of them did incessantly), instead of being interested or amused or whatever I used to be, I was pained. I thought about my own mother, how close we were, how much I missed her, how much I would have loved to pass on to a daughter or son what she gave me.

What brought this on? I had to figure it out. If I figure it out, I thought, I'll stop moping. I was wrong. It took more than understanding. It took acceptance. Mainly, it took time. I had to step back. Obviously, a big part of it was about being sixty. Sixty is when you pretty much know what has become of you and what hasn't. There are surprises, but after sixty the surprises are for sure not going to be babies, not your own.

My husband, no fool, pointed out something else to me: It's easy to be unhappy about a choice you've made when it's no longer a choice. The motherhood boat left years ago. Now I could drop (safely) to my knees at the shore and pound the sand in sorrow. We both knew that if the boat turned around to pick me up, I'd beg off. I found myself smiling at the thought. And then I took a good look at my husband, who— did I say this before?—is the world's greatest. It's embarrassing how happy we are, even after twenty-five years. A child would have changed things—maybe for the better, but I don't know that. I don't know what it would be like to have a child, period. I do know there is more to motherhood than That Look.

I found comfort in seeing children who were awful: a screaming kid on a plane, kids on drugs. I got to note with smug satisfaction that they weren't mine. But the fact was, most of the children I met were not screamers or drug addicts.

I continued to struggle with this nonmotherhood thing. The struggle ended when I stopped struggling. That is, I stopped trying so hard not to be sad. I realized—and accepted— that I'd always be sad about it. And I began to look around me. Who isn't sad about something missed in life? Or about something terrible that has been endured? Pollyanna (for whom, I confess, I've always had a weakness) showed up. Hey, she said, aren't you forgetting? You had breast cancer twice, and you're still breathing.

Actually, it was after one of those yearly oncologist visits that I felt a turn. You know how you climb up on the examining table and you think that you're probably okay, but you've had that same thought before when you weren't? Then you find out that you are, in fact, okay, and you fly home with new wings. And there's Miss Pollyanna again, perched on the sink, and she reminds you that aside from your good health, which you will never never take for granted, you're crazy about your husband and vice versa; you like your work. Why don't you focus on all of that and stop complaining?

So I did. 🍃

"Baby Blues" first appeared in *AARP Magazine*, July/August 2003.

Clutter, Cleaning, and Catharsis

by Nama Frenkel

O ne of the great shocks of adult life, for me, is that mattresses do not last forever. My husband Richard and I just faced this fact when looking at mattress prices. When we finally found a price that looked about right, the salesman said, "This is guest-room quality." My daughter was getting married in twenty days, so when we looked at our bank account, we gave up on new mattresses for a while. But the discomfort of the old mattress continued to bother my husband.

In fact, we do have another bed, a nearly new bed that Richard's parents gave us when they moved into their condo. It's been in the basement since Lydia, his daughter from a previous marriage, claimed it. When she was about fourteen, Lydia decided she wanted to move her room to the basement. She set up a "teen empire" down there. My mother made her a handmade quilt, she appropriated her favorites in my husband's art collection, and it was her world.

Lydia died of suicide about two-and-a-half years ago. The timing is impossible to forget because it happened the night of my son's engagement party. As I prepare for my daughter's wedding, the grief has hit me with torrential force. Until now,

I avoided it with a frenzy of fruitless activity designed to help other teens. My frantic efforts helped no one, while my inner life was as neglected as the room she used to occupy.

For the first year after she died, we left her bed untouched. No one even went in there. Once when the house was crowded, I tried to convince one of our young guests to sleep there. He said he'd rather sleep on the living room couch. Lydia's room wasn't a guest room, it was an unconscious mausoleum.

In a flurry of activity about a year ago, we decided to move the bed aside and put in a desk. I even tried to convince my husband to give the bed away to a young couple who had just moved into town. He refused. The bed stood against the wall, and the desk slowly accumulated junk. No one ever sat there.

Suddenly, the night before a Jewish holiday, my husband was determined that we should move Lydia's bed into our room. I was too stressed to imagine any changes, even for the better. I negotiated and pleaded. I gave in when a friend offered us a truck to take the mattresses to the dump.

When he took the bed upstairs, I wandered into the basement. I don't go there much. My daughter used to play "school" there, and my son lifted weights. Now my stepson does "projects," very messy projects with sawdust and many, many tools. My husband is a carpenter, so half the basement is taken up with his tools.

While we've avoided the basement, our fifteen-year-old has gone on his own way, piling up debris, tools, and Internet instructions in layers separated by dust and paint splatters.

When we first got married, I decided that the best way to get along was to split the basement into my zone and their zone and make no comments.

Now here I am among my husband's memorabilia. Everything is still in the boxes. Lydia's first of many suicide attempts distracted him from his unpacking when we first got married. Our history is not married: his things in his boxes, my things in my boxes.

My stepson has a workbench in the middle of it all. On it are fragments of unfinished science projects and an attempted hovercraft. If the experiments don't work, he just tosses them aside. His junk doesn't look very different from ours, undifferentiated by love or concern. Just lying there.

I looked at all that space, just sitting there collecting dust. Those rooms were once filled with laughter and whispered secrets. "Where did my life go?"

So I spent the entire day cleaning the basement. I carried out eight bags of garbage. I put the tools in order. There's more to do, but now there's loads of empty, clear space. Cleaning it up forces me to face the question, "What will we do with this big house now?"

As I cleaned, I noticed that a similar clutter had accumulated my mind. Since Lydia died, the pain, the loss, the anger, and the terror have slowly filled up my consciousness. Dusty half-empty boxes of feelings, too painful to touch, make it hard to see the heirlooms and the treasures. The pain is so familiar, it's part of the emotional furniture. Cleaning my "emotional" basement is degrading, heartbreaking. Where did all this mess come from? Where are the people who used to be sitting in those chairs?

Then I make up our new bed. My daughter comes in shining from the latest round of wedding errands. I can leave the basement for a while and prepare the food for the holiday guests. The room where we'll eat is hung with the roses I dried all year in the basement.

I hope I'll use the basement for more than rose-drying this year. I'd like to replace the memories of betrayal and indifference with loving and sharing. Next time, we'll clean the basement together and maybe bring our forgotten selves upstairs as well. 🎗️

My Ex-Husband's Baby

by Joyce Maynard

*I*t was the end of summer, and I had made a rare trip east from my home in California back to the town where I used to live for all the years of my marriage. I was picking up my youngest son, who'd been visiting his father. Twelve years had passed since I last spent a night in our old farmhouse, and now, on this particular trip, I was with a man I'd been dating for a number of months. My children's father had been living for the last six months or so with a young divorced woman who had three young children. He and I were not friends, but we had long since moved on with our lives.

Still, I can never make the turn onto our old road—spot the sign bearing my ex-husband's name only, now no longer mine—without a certain stab of sorrow. More than twenty years earlier, we celebrated our wedding at the house at the end of this road. Our three children were born on our bed there. I was here when I got the news my father had died, and—seven years later—the news that my mother was also dead. I planted lupine around the edges of the pond, by the house, and enough tomatoes in the garden to make a year's worth of spaghetti sauce, which I'd line up in rows on the pantry shelves. I could still remember the awful day I moved out, with a U-Haul truck full of my clothes and possessions, boxes of toys and children's books. I had bought this house when I was young with the dream of one day raising my family in it and, for twelve years, we did. No ambition had ever burned as bright for me as the dream of making a family here. No failure ever seemed so enormous or crushing as the realization that our life together was impossible and over.

Now I was back, though just for a moment. In previous times when I'd stopped by and my ex-husband was around, I was not invited in. This time, however, only my son was there, and so he threw the door open and I stepped in. I went no farther than the porch—the territory of the house itself feeling, now, like somewhere I was not supposed to go. But I didn't have to go beyond the porch to see it: a drawing of a face tacked to the wall and a single word, "Cerulean," scrawled across the top in the handwriting of my children's father.

I turned to my boyfriend at the time and grabbed his arm. "She's pregnant," I said.

"What are you talking about?" he asked me. "How can you know something like that?"

Twenty-three years earlier, that first day I came home from the doctor's with the news that we were having a baby (I was twenty-three, my husband twenty-five), we had stood on this porch, holding each other, dancing. That night we began talking about names. His own name was the kind parents of the fifties named their children in those days, and mine was only somewhat less common. But my artist husband wanted to name our baby something magical and amazing. Colors came to mind. Viridian green. Cerulean blue. Cerulean crimson. *Cerulean,* his favorite. I wasn't wild about the idea and, in the end, our baby was named Audrey. The two sons who followed were named after my husband's father and himself. Nothing out of the ordinary here.

We stood on the porch for no more than a minute. My son Willy came out with his duffel bag and jumped in the rental car. On the long drive from New Hampshire to New York City, we talked of many things—news of old friends, a camping trip he'd made, his plans for the new school year, and his excitement about stopping to see his older brother Charlie at his new dorm at NYU, where he had started as a freshman the week before. We were going to drop Willy off for a couple of hours to visit with Charlie on his own before heading out to the airport.

The whole drive down, I kept thinking about that piece of paper tacked to the wall. At forty-six, with three children nearly grown, and on the verge, finally, of reclaiming a certain freedom to pursue my own work and life apart from them, I should have been totally over babies—but I wasn't. For years after Willy's birth I had continued to believe there was another child in my future, if I could ever find the man to raise a child with, but I didn't. Long past the age when most of my friends had given all their baby books and toys and clothes away, I'd held on to mine, still hoping. I couldn't pass a pregnant woman on the street without a wistful feeling coming over me.

We dropped Willy off, and went to get a cup of coffee, to let the boys have a chance for a visit on their own. In the restaurant, I talked again about the drawing on the porch. "I can just tell," I said. "I felt it, the minute I walked into the house. There's a baby on the way. It's going to be born there, in the same place where mine were." Dennis, my boyfriend (a good man but not, in the end, the partner for me) looked at me as if I was crazy.

Two hours later, we picked up my son again. He said goodbye to his older brother and we headed off to the airport. In the car, heading out of the city, Willy drew in his breath in a way that made me know he had something difficult and significant to say.

"Dad told us not to tell you," he said. "But Charlie and I agreed you have a right to know. He and K. are going to have a baby."

I told him I knew that already. "I felt it when I was on the porch," I said.

My son was cautious talking about this. He knew me well enough to recognize that we were entering dangerous territory here. He had heard me railing enough over the years, about what I believed to be the unconscionable behavior of his father, who had chosen largely to ignore the financial responsibilities of parenthood, and certain others besides. Why did a man who had to ask me, when our son was nearing age two, where we kept the diapers, get to have another baby—at the age of forty-nine—when I, the one who'd taken care of them all these years, had no such option. As for my own baby prospects, I was too old. No longer fertile. Women younger than myself spent years seeking out specialists, thousands of dollars in pursuit of donor eggs and painful, humiliating procedures, all out of desperate longing to get what my ex-husband had managed to pull off with no greater difficulty, most likely, than had been necessary twenty-five years earlier when we'd conceived our daughter. Where was the fairness in that?

I didn't want my son to know how upset I was, so I kept my tone even and matter of fact, without (I hoped) betraying excessive interest. "That's going to be so much fun," I said.

"Imagine, after all these years of being the baby, you get to be a big brother."

Cautiously, Willy acknowledged his excitement. "They're hoping for a girl," he said. "But I think a brother would be just as great."

"You can't go wrong with babies," I said. "Both kinds are great."

"We weren't sure how you were going to take it," Willy said. "Charlie and I were afraid you might be pretty mad at Dad. I must say, this is a pleasant surprise, seeing you taking this so well."

"Oh, I'm happy for you," I told him. And I wanted to mean it.

Later, alone at last, came the tears. Not for any sense of missing my former husband, or jealousy that some other woman had him instead of me, or nostalgia for the old days. My tears were for what felt to me like the terrible, unfair laws of human biology: that the woman who so often did the work had only this surprisingly brief stretch of years to conceive their children in, while the men (who also missed out on episiotomies, stretch marks, and occasional midlife incontinence as a result of childbirth) could keep on firing off active sperm into their fifties, sixties, and beyond. They might not get to be around to dance at their children's weddings, or pay for college, but they could hand out the cigars at the hour of birth. While we, the women—no older than the men, just in possession of different equipment with a shorter shelf life—are relegated to the category of thick-waisted matrons, grandmothers, crones.

Partly, my grief and rage was for the baby I didn't get to have (the one I told myself I would have loved—Cerulean). Partly, it was about growing older, about the losses that come with age. Men can fool themselves about the aging process with younger girlfriends and babies. Women can only argue with the clock up to a point. We might get Botox injections or facelifts, or kill ourselves in the gym to keep our stomachs flat, but there's no fooling our eggs.

I hated what it was doing to me, the way thoughts of his baby were turning me into a bitter and resentful woman. I wanted to be generous, expansive, or simply oblivious. But at the oddest moments, I'd find myself thinking about it. And worrying.

"Now my children won't want to come spend Christmas with me anymore," I wept to a friend. "Who would, when they could go to a house with a baby? And then a toddler, and all those other great ages after that?

"I'm just me, alone here," I wallowed. (The boyfriend with whom I'd been that summer was gone now.) "Their dad can offer them a family."

A few times, I voiced my fears directly to my children's faces. "I know what's going to happen," I said. "You'll want to spend all your free time with the baby. I'll barely get to see you anymore."

"Mom," my son Charlie laughed. "You're losing it. I like babies fine, but I don't want them around all the time."

As usual, my daughter was the ultimate optimist. "The baby can be part of your life too, Mom," she offered. "Because we'll love him, and you love us, so we'll all love each other. You can be Aunt Joyce. You know how you love babies."

I wasn't sure how it would work, how the baby's father would explain why Aunt Joyce wasn't allowed in the house. But she was right about one thing. I do love babies.

He was born at home that spring—on the same bed where all three of my children had entered the world. The call came late one night, picked up on the message machine. Only my son Willy was around for me to tell, and he seemed interested and happy, though preoccupied, too, with the play he was acting in at the time, and a prom he was set to attend. I sent flowers to the baby's mother, *Warmest Wishes.* Then I lay down on the bed and had what I vowed would be my last good cry on this issue.

That summer, all three kids went back to New Hampshire to visit. The baby was very cute, they reported. They didn't get to hold him much yet, since he was nursing all the time. He had blond hair and amazing blue eyes, very faintly crossed. He also cried a lot. Often, I'd hear his voice in the background when I spoke to my kids on the phone.

That fall, I took off for a year of traveling in Central America. I fell in love and went to live on an island in Canada with the man I'd met the winter before—a man my age, with children nearly grown, like mine. Thoughts of my ex-husband's baby no longer haunted me. In fact, he barely crossed my mind, though when he did, there was nothing unpleasant about it.

Slowly, another life began to reveal itself to me: a life without babies. Not a better life than the one with them—I'll never say that—but an equally good life. And a better one, probably, for me.

Visiting with my daughter one day, she took out an envelope of photographs from a recent visit in New Hampshire with her father. She started to put a handful aside, then stopped. "You want to see the baby?" she asked. "A lot of people think he looks like Charlie."

So I reached for the photographs of Conor Cerulean. A beautiful heartbreaker of a baby, same as mine were. The kind of perfect baby you see in diaper commercials.

But here was the thing. Beautiful as he was—and I have yet to meet a baby I don't like—he also wasn't mine. He didn't tug at my heartstrings. The baby I missed, the baby I may, quietly, miss forever, wasn't this one. The baby I miss is the baby I didn't have with the man I didn't meet when I was still of an age to be having babies, the baby of my dreams. And maybe what I really miss is not even a baby at all, but the life I didn't have, with a baby's father. The dream of a family, with a mother and father and children all under the same roof. The marriage I had wanted so badly to be mine, that day we danced on the porch and tried out the sound of the name Cerulean.

The truth is, you don't get everything. In my case, I got three extraordinary children, work I love, good friends, and good health. And maybe a woman doesn't need young ovaries to get through midlife (though luck and courage come in handy). To be sure, a midlife love affair would not be possible with a baby in tow. I do call someone Baby, now and then. He's just a little older, that's all. 🙋

two

Starting the Voyage

I look forward to being older,
when what you look like becomes
less and less an issue and
what you are is the point.

~ Susan Sarandon

Hair Today, Gone Tomorrow

by Andrea Marcusa

"This is about saving the hair you have left," consoles my hairdresser, Danielle, as she runs her expert fingers through my hair. Slumped face-to-face with my shoulder-length locks, I assess their pitiful state: limp, thin, with scalp poking through around my temples. My mother's stinging words had brought me to the salon. "You used to have the most beautiful hair. Now it looks *terrible,*" she announced during my last visit. Mom sports short, unfussy ringlets, which solve a decades-old problem of fine, thinning hair. It's hard for Mom, who's eighty, to accept that my once-lush locks now suffer the same midlife crisis.

In our family, hairstyles take on an almost religious importance. My first hairstyling statement occurred at the age of three, when I sheared off half my honey-toned baby curls with my mother's sewing scissors. Horrified by the jagged result, Mom fixed my butchery by trimming off what was left, leaving me with a short pixie style. Free from the nuisance of combing out my tangles, Mom kept my hair short until I turned twelve, when I seized permanent control of my hair length . . . until now.

In high school, my best friend Jennifer would measure the lengths of her friends' tresses, asking, "Is it above or below your bra strap?" Mine was below, swinging around my shoulders and boldly cascading down to the middle of my back, setting off my eyes in flirtatious brown waves. Shorn of the pixie, I had shed my boyish looks. "Your hair is so thick and beautiful. I have such a gorgeous daughter," my mother had complimented. I think my robust mane helped her feel better about her own withering locks, which already were streaked with gray and visibly thin.

Although pretty in her own way, Mom had always lived in the shadow of her fair-haired mother, a Latvian beauty who'd dazzled my Irish grandfather with her azure eyes and long golden tresses. A few years later, as my mom neared fifty, she cropped her hair to within an inch of her scalp to mask the thinning. Her short gray curls and scrubbed ruddy complexion suited her natural beauty, a contrast she'd cultivated years earlier in reaction to my grandmother's bleached hair and painted face. At the time, I dismissed my mother's fate as her unfortunate genetic destiny. I believed my thick waves were inherited from my father's side of the family and that they would forever remain full and healthy, as his had. But thin hair had already plagued two generations of *women*.

By the time my grandmother turned eighty, she had lost most of her hair. She wore a matted ash-blond wig shaped in the style of a 1920s flapper. Bobby pins, affixed right below her ears, trained the synthetic mane to frame her now jowly neckline. It lay slightly lopsided on her head, a counterpoint to her imperfect eye (her vanity ran so deep, she refused to use eyeglasses) and lip liner. But Grandmother's bald-headedness never held her back. Widowed at fifty-nine, she dated and partied right up to the day she died thirty years later, dressed for a night out in an aquamarine knit suit, salmon mousse lipstick, and her artificial blond bob. My hairdresser peers at me in the mirror, resting her hand on my shoulder. I see her thick straight brown hair fall to the middle of her back, while mine dusts my shoulders in wispy anorexic strands. "Your hair is healthy," Danielle reassures. "It's common for it to thin as you get older. You're not going bald."

I first noticed the hair loss at about the same time gray strands started streaking my part. Monthly color treatments were supposed to help both conditions, masking my gray and adding body. They did maintain my brown hue, but my hair felt sparse. Patches of white scalp showed through around my temples. Determined to fight my familial fate, I turned to science, swallowing hair-growth-enhancing vitamins and applying tonics to encourage regrowth. No change. "You know," explains Danielle, "about a third of all women experience thinning from the time they turn thirty. When they reach forty, some only have two hairs where there were once five."

As she picks up my brown strands and lets them flop back feebly onto my head, Danielle suggests, "Layering your hair will give it a fuller look." At only twenty-four, Danielle puts me in her mother's generation. "The short style will lift your entire face. My mom keeps her hair short now too." As Danielle speaks, my heart sinks as I imagine myself with a "sensible" cut sported by women wearing bifocals and fighting thickening waistlines; surely this is not the look of a woman who not long ago could get an invitation to dinner with a swing of her mane. Cutting off my hair has always symbolized crossing the threshold into middle age. When I was in my twenties, I wondered why attractive sexy women sheared off their hair when they reached their forties. I swore to keep mine long.

Short hair at forty was defeminizing, an overt expression of a woman's waning sexuality. A layered bob and comfortable shoes signaled that life had worn the woman out, like a discontinued old car or kitchen appliance. In my twenties, I didn't understand that cutting off your hair is a way of making the best of where you are in life, rather than holding on to the past. Nor did I realize that many of the youthful, attractive, upbeat women I admired with short cuts were themselves well past the age of forty. "Okay, cut it off," I surrender. "You'll look much better," Danielle reassures. I think about how freely my mother dives into the ocean, and how my grandmother danced the night away. I hear the scissors cutting as I watch my feathery wisps drift to the floor. For the first time in thirty years, my hair barely covers my ears. I examine myself in the mirror. Not bad! My hair looks full and lush; after the blow dryer and styling brush, even the thinning areas have disappeared.

As Danielle predicted, I look younger, sexier. The style will take some getting used to. But if a long life span, like hair loss, is all in the genes, I'm guaranteed at least forty-five more years of living. Ample time to bounce back. And to love the new me. ❧

The Joy of Not Bleeding

by Shoshana Bat-Zvi

m I the only woman on the face of the planet who eagerly wished for menopause to come sooner rather than later? Am I the only one who looked forward to the literal meaning of the word—the cessation of the cycle of monthly bleeding? Menstruation did not seem to be too overwhelming for most of my friends. Of course, they complained of cramps, bloating, or some of the other common discomforts. But in addition to sharing those complaints, for me the onset of regular bleeding was the beginning of years—decades really—of extreme blood loss, anemia, fear of embarrassment and hemorrhage, and an ongoing obstacle to leading an unconstricted life.

I did not realize at first that almost from the outset, my bleeding was abnormally heavy. As the situation worsened over the years, affecting my travel plans, my ease in sleeping over at someone's home or my ability to walk or engage in other activities, menstruation seemed to be taking over my life. So perhaps it was only natural and normal that I should look forward with the greatest anticipation to the menopause, the end of the monthly flow that was draining my body and sapping my strength.

If my heart had been set on motherhood, my reactions would surely have been different. I would have been willing to put up with almost anything for the sake of creating life inside my womb. But from an early age, much as I loved children, I knew that motherhood was not for me. Instead, I cherished the role of benevolent aunt, someone who relished playing with her siblings' kids, boosting their self-esteem, and perhaps teaching them something before sending them merrily on their way, back to their parents. Even so, however, I confess that on occasion, I experienced the menstrual flow as a monthly shedding of my unborn, or never-to-be-born children. This perception surfaced in particular when intense labor-like pains only resulted in the "birth" of clots—masses of even more blood.

I don't remember exactly when menstruation emerged in my consciousness. I do recall one early preadolescent scene, however. I was in a public restroom with my mother when I noticed a small box, some sort of vending machine on the wall. "Oh, look, Mommy," I exclaimed. "They sell napkins. And they're even sanitary. Can we get some?" It was at that point, I believe, that my mother decided to have THE TALK with me.

Little did I suspect how crucial those dispensers would become to my existence. Had I really had foresight, I would have bought thousands of shares in Kimberly Clark Corporation, the makers of Kotex. I remember that my friends and I spent some hours perusing a little brochure put out by Kotex. It painted a rosy picture (no pun intended) of physical maturity. As it turned out, most of those happy, upbeat descriptions would not apply to my life, my cycles, my protective needs.

I have lived through many changes, advances some might say, in the field of feminine protection. I started out using pads

hooked up to belts. One side of the pad had a blue line, signi-
fying that it was the side to be worn away from the body. A
friend of mine accidentally put a pad on backwards and worried that somehow that blue line would compromise her
immune system and be harmful to her health. Years later, we
had self-adhesive pads—a great innovation—allowing us to dispense with the hated belts. Later still, we were given pads with
wings, maxi-pads, super pads, thin pads, oval pads, and a
number of other variations on a theme. There was only one
problem. None of them worked for me.

A breakthrough of sorts occurred one day when a close
friend suggested that I wear two pads at a time. She was right.
That certainly helped for a while. But then what about
overnight or other occasions requiring more protection? Suffice
it to say that I worked my way up to wearing four super pads
together. I won't go into the gory placement details, but I will
say that even this meticulous construction was ineffective.
Also, I'm amazed that I could walk at all without developing
some strange, loping gait.

Despite my fortress of cotton, how many mornings did I
awake in fear of making any sudden movement at all? I'd lie
there, perfectly still, knowing that for the moment, all was
well. But from the sensations in my uterus, it was clear that
any movement, to the right or the left, would release a sudden
cataract of blood, staining me, my pajamas, the linen, and perhaps, the bed pad or mattress. I recall the night that I slept over
at the apartment of a married friend, whose only available
accommodation was a couch, a white couch, in her living
room. I think the stain came out.

But that was not always the case. I ended up throwing
some garments away because I could not clean them well

enough to give them to a thrift shop. My black skirt became my constant companion. You can never have too many black skirts. Of course, a pastel or white one was simply out of the question for me. Blue was not good enough, either, I discovered. I remember well the time that I wore a blue print dress to a luncheon, where I sat for several hours with no opportunity to change my protective pads. When I arose from my place to go to the buffet table for dessert, a sudden whoosh of blood, which I could feel, of course, came pouring forth, soiling the back of my dress. Two kind friends stood behind me from then on and later provided an unusual escort as I walked home. They were ladies-in-waiting to my queen, walking several paces behind me.

Let's see. Other memorable moments. The time at the wedding when I danced, and I should not have. The stain on that purple dress, which washed out, and the stain on the fancy chair, which did not. A friend predicted that it could never be removed. That brings up an interesting question. How are you supposed to let the caterer know that you've probably just ruined an expensive chair? For that matter, Emily Post never discussed what to say to the driver when you are getting out of a cab at the emergency room and you notice that you've soiled the back seat of the taxi. What is the approved way to turn down the offer of a ride from someone who has a fancy car with beautiful white leather seats?

One of the more memorable days of my life involved an extended bus trip from Ohio to New York. There was a bathroom, of sorts, on the bus, and a brief visit to a truck stop along the way, so that the journey itself was just bearable. Then we arrived at New York City's Port Authority terminal, the site of restroom accommodations that one would not ordinarily choose. I was pretty desperate for a change of protection, but I could not bring myself to use those facilities which, at the time, were frequented mainly by the homeless. My uncle was supposed to be picking us up soon and taking us to his home in New Jersey, so I thought I could wait. It turned out that he was a little late in coming, but that was okay. In the meantime, I had my first "Welcome to New York" moment. A man carrying a purse went running by me on his mad dash out to the street, followed by screams of "Stop, thief!" There was no way that I could help to pursue him, and I never did find out how the chase ended.

Meanwhile, my uncle showed up and led us to his car, necessitating a walk of some distance to the adjacent parking structure. I could at least sit down during the next phase of the trip, while we drove to Newark Airport to pick up another relative. When we finally pulled up at the airport, I was pretty anxious to take care of my sanitary needs. I hurried into the building and followed the signs and the pictographs, walking down long concourses until I finally spied a door with "Women" written on it. But, as I started to step inside, I was stopped by a temporary barrier informing me that the room was being cleaned and serviced. I was directed to another restroom at the opposite end of the terminal. I decided to hang in there for the rest of the car ride rather than undertake a marathon sprint down the massive hallways of the terminal. Somehow, I made it to the safety of my uncle's home without anything publicly amiss.

Over the years, the cleaning of restrooms was not the only thing to stand between me and the protection I needed. How about that evening when I was taking a night class at the local university, and I suddenly, urgently, needed some supplies?

I started walking downhill to the student union. Halfway there, I bumped into an old friend, someone I hadn't seen in many years. She stood there, smiling, happy to see me. I was flattered, I guess, by her attention and it was hard to interrupt her monologue, as she brought me up to date on what she was studying, gave me her phone number, and asked if we could get together sometime. I think I babbled on rather incoherently for a few minutes before running those last few yards into the bathroom, only to find that the sanitary pad dispenser was empty. I had only a few minutes until my class began. I ran down to the student store and bought a small container of baby powder. I think I calculated that it might just help me get through the evening, thanks to its capacities to absorb and cover any unpleasant odors. Desperate times call for desperate measures, I have discovered firsthand. Even now, I clearly remember that episode many years ago in a small Israeli village, when I was reduced to buying a package of cotton wool to tide me through a day and night. Trust me, it does not do the trick.

All of these scenes from the past come flooding back to me (again, no pun intended) along with the emotions that accompanied them. They say that the human mind has no memory of pain, since such constant re-experiencing of it would make life unbearable. But the memories of shame, fear, and discomfort are quite vivid indeed. So are some of the relevant lessons of my childhood. I distinctly hear the voice of my high school gym teacher during one of her first-aid lessons: "What are the three emergencies that require immediate attention? Bleeding, stopped breathing, and poisoning." Years later, when I found myself at an emergency room triage desk, describing the symptoms of my menorrhagia, I learned that my teacher was right. Once I spoke the magic words, "I am bleeding," I was led down the hall and attended to at once, unlike some of the other would-be patients who were left to languish in the waiting room.

At first I went to male gynecologists. I don't think I had much choice in those days. And they were pretty good at what they did, although I knew they could never really understand what I was experiencing. One did express his feelings, though, after I told him about the dancing-at-the-wedding incident. "If I had soiled a nice gown, I think I would do something about it," he said. I guess his words and my desperation got through to me, because he convinced me to have my first D&C. Afterward, he called me and said, "We'll have to talk. You have a lot of tumors." I walked around for two days, until the time of my appointment, worrying that I had a malignancy. Only then did he explain about fibroids, completely benign growths, apologizing that "I'm not very good on the telephone."

The female gynecologist that I later went to was not a wonder worker, either, but she clearly knew what I was talking about. She even shared with me the story of her friend, who suffered from a problem similar to mine. Her friend was making a corporate presentation one day, when she suffered a sudden, massive hemorrhage, her blood actually spilling onto the floor. "But she was lucky," my doctor said. "She passed out so she didn't have to worry about being embarrassed." What a vivid picture she painted in my mind! I could only agree that in such circumstances, losing consciousness would probably be a good thing.

Those of us who have experienced a low red-blood count at one time or another are made to worry about the consequences of such a depleted state. While I was anemic for so many years, living on iron supplements, I thought of myself as a car that was low on motor oil. I joked to friends that I was "down a quart." But it was not a laughing matter. A physician who wanted to spur me into taking some action to resolve my problem told me, "If you don't do anything about this, you're going to have a cyanotic episode and wake up in the hospital."

But I kept hanging in there, hoping against hope that if I could wait only another few years, nature would take its course and I would be free at last. Meanwhile, I suffered. In addition to my bleeding problems, the oral liquid iron temporarily stained my teeth. And the injections of iron, not in my arm, discolored the surrounding skin for what seemed like years.

I was not able to hold on until the bleeding stopped on its own. My problem actually worsened with age. I finally decided to undergo an outpatient procedure, a hysteroscopy, which was unsuccessful. Then another. I ended up having three hysteroscopies, none of them resolving my problem. The last one was even marred by a complication that required a laparoscopy. The final hysteroscopy, with ablation, was the most invasive procedure of all. During it, the lining of my uterus was destroyed, forever putting an end to my ability to bear a child.

As after previous procedures, I viewed the videotape of that surgery in my doctor's office some days after it took place. It is strange to view the self as a number of organs and vessels, rather than as a thinking and self-reflecting totality. By seeing those internal structures and discussing their functions and imperfections with my physician, my focus shifted, at least temporarily, to my physiological self. But I am so much more than that. There is so much more to my identity than "I bleed, therefore I am."

Even the endometrial ablation did not succeed in controlling my bleeding. It became increasingly clear that I had no choice but to proceed with a hysterectomy, which I had put off for so many years. "You've already gone the extra mile," my doctor told me. "You've gone the extra thousand miles." Her office was ready to nominate me for the Golden Uterus award for just that reason. I finally decided to go ahead with the operation. I approached the surgery with great anxiety, despite my doctor's promise that this would be easier than some of my earlier procedures. Happily, she was right. The operation went well, and I was cured at last.

It helped me to think of the hysterectomy as the ultimate C-section, in which I was delivered of a very unhealthy uterus. In addition to multiple, massive fibroids, the doctors found that I had a huge, heavy uterus, thick of wall and tissue. In a way, I'm sorry that I never got to see it once it was excised, so I could have a clear image of it, my own organ yet my enemy within.

Weeks after the surgery, with the stabilization of my hemoglobin and red cell count, I began to have color in my face. Many people told me that my color had returned, but I knew that it had not been there in the first place. I went out and bought a white skirt to wear with confident pleasure. I began to take brisk walks whenever the spirit moved me. By removing the source of my blood, symbolically regarded as the essence of life, I had come to live a richer, fuller life. For me, it is wonderful not to bleed. 🦋

Facing the Fire

by Nancy Andres

Eleven years ago, when I was fifty-one, a smoldering volcano from deep inside erupted and caught me by surprise. When I tuned into my body's messages, it transformed my life.

In my circle of women friends, I was first to experience red-hot-poker waves of searing heat. The hormonal shifts were sudden, shooting from my scalp to the soles of my feet and drenching me to my core. I was infuriated, because it felt as though my body was betraying me, suddenly and shockingly.

* * *

1991. I need a mother, I think, but mine is dead. She died when I was forty-two. Chronic depression and asthma permeated many of my mother's days, yet Mom gave the best hugs. I miss her and her warm embrace. There are only a few women in my family, and they are closed-mouthed. When I ask one aunt about her "Change of Life" she says, "I don't remember." Another says it's not a subject she cares to discuss.

• • •

My reverie draws me deeper into the past to a June day in 1953. One week after my twelfth birthday, I awaken and lay in bed contentedly, until I realize I'm wet and sticky between my legs. There's blood on the sheet, and I rip it off. "Mom," I shout. "Look!"

My mother pushes me into the bathroom, hands me a belt and a pad and says, "Clean yourself up. Put this Kotex on."

I wrestle with the ends of the sanitary napkin and don't know which end to attach. I blush and timidly motion for help. A few hours later, I thank God, I haven't bled to death. Confusion and fear make me stutter, "What happened . . . to you . . . at my age?"

"I got through it," Mom says as she walks away.

• • •

During the fall of my twelfth year, I sprout to five foot one and tower over my mother's head. Her top-heavy 185 pounds make a giant shadow on the sidewalk, so big it engulfs mine. We walk down Park Avenue, in the midst of the business section of Long Beach, New York, an East Coast city, toward the corset shop. My mouth drops open as Mom orders a custom-made brassiere. The standard ones don't come in her size. In my secret heart, I promise myself I'll never become as mis-shapen and fat as she is, and my harsh judgment makes me squirm.

Another question, "What did you look like when you married Dad?" receives a grumble and, "That's enough."

. . .

1992. Three months after my first hot flash, during my yearly checkup, my gynecologist rattles off symptoms. "Irregular periods, intermittent staining, and/or the complete cessation of menstruation."

The doctor bows her head and scribbles my weight and height on the chart. A hormone level blood test and a bone density test are prescribed—only after I insist. I've read every health publication I can find and want a marker for bone density and hormone levels. It will help me evaluate my choices and options for the future.

I try to act confident, but my vulnerable core shrinks as I sit across the desk from my gynecologist. I'm a baby bear, sitting there in a wee little chair, and feel just like my twelve-year-old self. I wish my doctor would look up or smile. Before I can ask when to expect the test results, my physician is gone. Bedside manner is nonexistent in these quarters and I leave the office, still hungry for a dose of compassion. Needless to say, shopping for a new doctor is at the top of my to-do list.

Heart palpitations, chills and sweats, and cycles of crying and giddiness grip me by surprise and take shape in dreams as monsters, earthquakes, and flames. I lose sleep and often feel tired and edgy. My body is my teacher, and it warns me to cut back on obligations and limit contact with people who are a drain on my serenity. I want and need peace.

. . .

Several pieces of my menopausal puzzle come together, as I search for clarity. Serendipitously, I discover a women's issues seminar at Omego Institute in Reinbeck, New York, with

Dr. Christiane Northrup, a holistic physician and noted speaker. Our group participates in a ceremony to invite our sisters, aunts, mothers, daughters, friends, and female ancestors into our circle, and my shoulders drop several inches.

When I read Northrup's book, *Women's Bodies, Women's Wisdom,* it rings true and validates me at a deep level. In the chapter called "Steps for Healing," Northrup explains how unresolved childhood woundings such as incest, chronic illness in a parent, or having a parent abandon the family may show itself in hot flashes.

Of course, I admit to myself. My body is revealing its truth and its own language, a dialect of submerged and exploding anger, hurt, and fear.

Before this season in my life, I placate and appease my dad and act as though his sexist jokes don't offend me. I visit him, even though there is a drunken glaze over his eyes. I am the one to initiate phone calls, remember birthdays, and arrange family gatherings. When I stop tap-dancing around my dad, it feels like graduation, the metamorphosis of a people-pleasing nice girl into a grown-up woman.

"You turned so negative," Aunt B says.

"Sorry you feel that way," I reply.

"Not today," becomes a favorite expression of mine, as I bow out of a grocery run for a neighbor. My power of concentration easily short-circuits, especially by 4 P.M. New calming and grounding self-care practices like yoga and meditation are substituted for busyness and provide the essential time I need to be with myself.

Susan Weed's book, *Menopausal Years: The Wise Woman Way,* helps me identify my super-sensitivity to smells, bright lights, noise, and commotion as menopausal characteristics. Weed outlines and references herbal allies like black cohosh and vitex berries. These herbs work for me, at different times, to give me a sense of equilibrium. I find that what helps at some point may have to be adjusted or eliminated at another. I stay vigilant and continually check in with myself.

Hormone replacement therapy—HRT—is ruled out. I won't be increasing my risk of breast cancer and am relieved my bone density is way above average. I choose to witness my menopausal symptoms, not mask them.

I wake in the middle of the night and cocoon and reread *Necessary Losses,* by Judith Viorst. It helps me grieve the loss of my childbearing years and mourn and release the fantasy of having had a wholesome childhood.

My husband is a staunch supporter and backs my decision to leave my travel-agency job to re-evaluate my priorities. It's the right time for me to get into therapy, with a caring professional trained in the family disease of alcoholism. A handlettered plaque with the Serenity Prayer and a delicate milkglass vase of baby roses welcomes me into the safe room Marilyn, my counselor, creates. I explore and integrate the trauma of childhood sexual abuse and the effects of growing up in an alcoholic home. I breathe through my pain and stay grounded in the here and now, by stamping my foot. I confess in a session that my hormones are quickly moving me to the grave. Yes, we laugh aloud. Menopause is a life passage, but not the final one!

The hot and sweaty midnight heat is fuel for a budding career in freelance writing. Instead of agonizing over lost sleep and counting trips to the bathroom, I'm inspired to pen a memoir and cook delectable dishes like vegetarian stuffed cabbage and strudel. My mate dons flannel pajamas as I fling open the winter windows to let in the cooling air.

• • •

As I look back, I realize my skepticism and anxiety were understandable. The articles and advertisements in newspapers, television, and magazines in 1991, 1992, and 1993 highlighted the increased risk of heart attacks and stroke, osteoporosis, vaginal dryness, and wrinkling during menopause. Most doctors of the day recommended HRT. Those I spoke with told me if I didn't follow this course of action, I'd have to contend with fragile bones and a decrepit body and mind.

• • •

An unmet need for an interchange of ideas and support motivates me to share the ride. I hug others and myself by formulating and facilitating a workshop, "Recipes for Menopause and Beyond," at the Long Beach Public Library.

It's exhilarating to gather with other menopausal women to role-play. Some of us confess we're afraid of losing our looks or losing lovers to younger women. Others admit they've fallen out of love or want to turn their lives upside down and live alone. We discuss soy recipes and foods and supplements helpful during menopause and beyond, those rich in vitamin E, calcium, magnesium, and vitamin D. We practice pelvic floor exercises for improved muscle control and enhanced sexual pleasure.

A questionnaire—a follow-up to the workshop—indicates 90 percent of those who attended feel less isolated as a result of the workshop, and several commented that for the first time since they started menopause, they feel "heard and empowered."

. . .

I recount the distance I've traveled and realize that from the time I was nine, stuffing myself with high-carb food like spaghetti and whole loaves of bread temporarily dulled my loneliness. Mom, Dad, and I used food as a stand-in for the nurturing and communication we didn't know how to do.

My process taught me that self-care doesn't mean self-indulgence or blaming, and I've let go of the past by forgiving my parents for their mistakes. During menopause, I pay close attention to my food choices and take long walks on the board-walk to reduce stress and promote health. My efforts pay off because they moderate my symptoms.

. . .

A new wrinkle or line on my face may bring momentary regret. Nevertheless, I appreciate "all" of me. The proactive stance I took during menopause helped me heal ancient wounds and foster greater self-assurance. Today I see with wiser, crone eyes, the eyes of a Post-Menopausal Goddess. My journey through menopause brought me to a place of renewed vitality and joy, and I celebrate my life passage. ❧

Passing the Hormonal Torch

by Jennifer Delahunty Britz

*I*f I were to imagine a hell on earth it would be the swimsuit department—that place you go when you have no choice left but to swim in your underwear.

Last week I took my two teenage daughters on our annual outing to hell. They plucked shimmery triangular pieces of cloth off the displays and approached the dressing rooms. I grabbed the only number with a skirt. We all emerged from behind our separate curtains, shy and cautious. For a nanosecond, we stood in the three-way mirror—three women at different stages of the hormonal drama that is a woman's life. I'm forty-two and perimenopausal, the confusing prelude to menopause. My fourteen-year-old is fully grown and has entered the mysterious world of menses. My youngest daughter, nearly twelve, is just on the cusp of riding what teenage boys call "the cotton pony." Looking at themselves in that dressing room mirror, my daughters saw nothing but problems, I'm sure. I, on the other hand, saw lithe curves, breathtakingly long legs, impatient breasts. And as I looked in the mirror at myself—I'll spare you the description of fleshy lobes extruded by tight straps—I saw a woman whose body has betrayed her just when she needs it most.

How can it be, I asked myself as I looked at our images, that my daughters are experiencing full-blown puberty at precisely the same time I'm leaving the ranks of those with fertile wombs? It's definitive proof that God is not a woman. If she were, she would have worked out better timing.

This cruel coincidence of hormonal comings and goings has created a contentious atmosphere beneath our roof. My cheery "Good morning" is greeted with a surly look that says, "What's it to ya?" But it's no wonder we're grumpy. Our hormones dominate our every waking—and especially our sleeping—moments. While my daughters awaken in the middle of the night, their sheets twisted and damp from dreaming about Brian or Andrew or Ross, across the hall I wake up soaked in the sweat of longing for my two lost loves, estrogen and progesterone. Although I infrequently think about sex with my husband, my daughters are walking—or shall I say strutting—the halls of middle school thinking of little else but sexual activity with males of their generation.

Because I've chosen to resist HRT (hormone replacement therapy—I prefer the acronymal definition of "Horrible Rotten Timing" instead), my herbal cure consists of vitamin E (8 mg a day), vitamin B_6 (1.3 mg a day), 3 grams daily of evening primrose, and generous helpings of soy isoflavone, black cohosh, and natural progesterone cream. My daughters, who have suddenly become poster children for why the world needs more dermatologists, have been prescribed a potent cocktail of Cleosin T, Benzac, erythromycin, and Theramycin Z for their faces. It seems that our hormones, meant to serve us—to keep our skin lustrous and our eyes shining—have turned alien and are eating us, their hosts.

That's not to say that all these changes have been negative. My daughters' hormones have made them accomplished artists. Their palettes? Their own faces. At thirteen, my oldest asked me to buy her something called "concealer." What was she talking about? (I'm a makeup innocent who didn't shave my legs until I had a baby and only then out of respect for the obstetrician.) She dabs the white gook beneath her eyes with as much care and precision as Vermeer did his oils on canvas. My younger daughter spends hours before her mirror twiddling her lustrous auburn locks into hairdos that rival those of Princess Leia. They become absorbed in their work. When they ride beside me in the car, both of my daughters reposition the side mirror so they can steal glances at themselves all the way home. I catch them sucking in their cheeks, smoothing their eyebrows, turning their chins this way, then that, measuring and evaluating, asking the eternal question, "Am I pretty enough?"

I remember how hard it is to be the owner of new hormones. I remember the grayness of some days and the blissful ecstasy of others. I remember the ache of longing, longing, longing for that nameless something or someone who never arrives. I scribbled for hours in notebooks trying to puzzle out the world, puzzle out myself. And I fought my mother in the way that hurt her most—I avoided her. At all costs. She couldn't possibly understand me, so why bother? If I'd only known, she was probably watching me with the same conflicted mix of awe, envy, pride, and empathy that I now intensely feel for my own daughters.

My calm husband is watching this transformation from a distance. His testosterone may be on the decline, but that loss isn't bloating his breasts or adding unwanted flesh (an average of eleven pounds for every menopausal woman). He watches

the hysterical encounters among the women in his life—
"You've been in the bathroom for three days. Shall I forward
your mail?"—with a calm bemusement. While we three head
off into uncharted waters, he sails the exact same boat, the
calm captain reclining on the couch with a book. My "change"
is, unfortunately, just one more in a series of hormonal the-
atrics he has witnessed in our twenty years of marriage. Act I:
The surge of lust. Act II: The primal urge to bear children. Act
III: The whole mammalian experience—birthing, nursing,
weaning, etc. And now, at last, we've arrived at the final act.
"Please, no encores," he must be thinking.

And though the timing, quite frankly, stinks—I'm exiting
the house of hormones just as my daughters enter—I must
admit there's a poetic rightness to it. It's a kind of transfusion,
a passing of the hormonal torch from me to them, another natural step in what the poet Kathleen Norris calls "the long
goodbye" between mother and child. I birthed you, now it's
your turn.

But not before you're ready, I add firmly. Just as I thought I
was done fretting about birth control, just as my final eggs are
dropping, conception has returned as a top-of-mind concern.

Only this time, it's my daughters' bottoms that are on the
top of my mind. ❧

Three Calls

Barbara Scott

I held the receiver so long without dialing that I started to hear that repeated message: "If you want to make a call, please hang up . . ." This was followed by a loud ugly buzz, no doubt intended to alert someone in the house that an old person had fallen unconscious while attempting to dial 911.

I wasn't so old—forty-nine—and though not entirely unconscious, I had, after all, let the receiver dangle in my hand, avoiding the logical next step on the road to healing myself. It wasn't a 911 call, but it was a near thing.

Eight months ago Zack had left me. The woman he took to what had been our little cabin retreat in southern Spain was not precisely a floozy, but she was younger than me—thirty-four—and fertile. I knew Zack had made his choice. Ours was a childless marriage. He didn't want to experience his own decline by looking at an old woman.

This sent me on my downhill slide. And precipitated early menopause. Like a rape victim, I felt secretly ashamed, sure I had failed somehow. Leaving everything I had put together in Europe with Zack, I came back to North Carolina and settled in a tourist town in the mountains where I could pursue mindless employment in a health food store and avoid seeing anyone who'd ever known me before. The latter wasn't too difficult because Zack had circumscribed my social life so that after eighteen years of marriage I had hardly any friends left. Or so I thought.

I lived in an ever-tightening vortex of loneliness, counting every white hair and hot flash. I had an almost irresistible urge to weep in public. This effectively kept me from going out any-where, even to a women's singing group that could have been a saving grace. Instead, I watched television—mostly lush costume dramas on PBS—and ate popcorn for supper almost every night.

At the health food store, I was surrounded by vigorous youngsters who treated me with respect—which only made me feel more pitiful.

One day I literally bumped into a pamphlet stand by the coffee machine at work. I pulled out something to read on my break. It described being depressed in vivid enough detail to scare me into action. One strategy the pamphlet recommended was to get in contact with people you care about—people who would listen.

It seemed simple enough. But Zack had pulled the social rug out from under me in his need for total control. So who to call?

Joyce was the first name that came to mind. I knew that she hadn't moved in about ten years, which was how long it had probably been since I talked to her last. We'd corresponded some after I followed Zack across Europe and parts of Africa, but inevitably we'd lost touch.

I didn't know it was going to take so much in the way of guts to phone her. When I finally did what the phone suggested—hung up and redialed—I was amazed to hear Joyce across the states, her voice the same as I remembered, with a little thrill of happiness as she realized it was really me.

"This is amazing! I was just thinking about you!"

"No!"

"Yes! You know why?"

"No!"

"I have this cat . . ."

"I know, Mr. Benjamin."

"No, um, Mr. Benjamin died. A while back. It was very sad. But I have a new kitten—can you guess what I called it?"

This wasn't as odd a question as it seemed. We used to joke about how Joyce always named new things after old ones—she had Plant, Mr. Plant, and Plant Mama, and for a while, two fish named Goldy and Goldier.

"Um, Mrs. Benjamin?"

The laugh shook the phone; we were in the same zone again. "No, but you're close—it's Little Benjamin." We savored the moment, piled a few more memories on it, and finally she asked, "But why are you calling? I heard about you and Zack, by the way—but what, Barbara, what happened?"

"Oh, Joyce, I can't talk about it. I feel like I got run over by a bus. Now I'm in damn menopause and I'm flashing and flushing and I look like hell."

"Everybody has to go into menopause. You know, it's not a disease."

"But it's proof."

"That what? That you're wiser and cooler than ever?"

"Yeah, sure. I'm sorry, Joyce, but that seems pretty hard to believe right now. And I feel so lonely—I can't imagine ever being in love again. It's like—I'm just drying up and I'm gonna blow away."

Joyce was quiet for a minute and then she said, "Barbara, are you seeing a counselor? Or a doctor?"

"You're it so far for counseling."

"Well, I'm pretty damned good, but I'm not good enough. You need to talk to someone who can help you process your feelings."

"I've kind of, like, gotten out of going out at night . . ."

"Well, there's lots of things happening in the daytime, Barbara. Anyway, what does the doctor say about your menopause?"

"He—well, it's kind of hard to talk to him. He wants me to take pills, and I don't know . . ."

"Barbara, you want one good piece of advice?"

"That's why I called—more than one, if you got it."

"Get a *woman* doctor."

The conversation wound down after nearly an hour, and I knew I'd never lose Joyce again. I'd always have her by the phone cord that binds. Joyce gave me Kelsa's number, and I plunged on. This time there was no pause for a recorded scolding.

Kelsa too, as if by prearrangement, was home and happy to hear from me. She correctly perceived that I was hoarse; she and I had been singing partners at one time in the paisley days. "You need to start visualizing."

"Oh, Lord, what new trendy thing is that?"

"You work in a health food store—don't you ever listen to anybody there or read anything on the racks?"

"Actually, this call is a result of finally reading something."

"When you get off the phone, lie down and visualize your physical difficulty and then think of how to feel well again. You're putting this on yourself. Sinuses mean you feel like you have to punish yourself. And you can visualize your outcomes for menopause, too."

"How can there be any outcome for menopause—except old age and death?"

"Barbara, dear, menopause is only the beginning of a new life. It's like shedding an old skin. Hey, that would be a cool visualization!"

Kelsa explained her own visualization technique in gracious detail and then gave me a number where she thought I could reach Rosie. We both knew how hard it was to track Rosie down. It would be a long shot, but I was on a roll.

Rosie listened to my outpourings, which by now were starting to sound different as I listened to myself. In place of despair, I had a strong surge of anger and instead of hopelessness, I was beginning to feel that life, even in menopause, might be worth recouping.

Rosie honed in on my work situation. "You used to be an editor, like me. What happened?"

"I dunno, Rose—I just thought, well, health food, healthy, simple. Nothing too high-powered."

"You're undervaluing yourself. Besides, it sounds like your supervisor is a jerk." He was, in fact. "Well, you were married to a jerk and he dominated you and here you are feeling like a warmed-over dog supper. Why let another jerk lean on you? Why not quit your job?"

"Well, like, money?"

"Don't you have any money put aside?"

"Not much . . . maybe a few weeks' worth. But I was kind of thinking about getting a roommate." This was a white lie— the thought had crossed my mind at high speed once, but I was too jammed up to consider acting on it.

"That's perfect! Find another woman, someone our age, someone going through changes like you are. Share the poop!"

"Are you serious?"

Rose laughed. "Actually, I was. Quit the job, get a boarder, and opportunities will open up. You have my personal guarantee!"

Three weeks later I had cleared out my spare room, and my new boarder Avril moved in. I found a woman doctor who encouraged visualizing and gave me a hug when I left her office. She didn't have fixed ideas about treatment for symptoms of menopause; she gave me some reading material and told me to get back to her.

I began to stop blaming either Zack or menopause for every little thing that had pushed me toward the edge. I was untangling the strands of pain and confusion. Some of them were hard to look at, but others gave me creative impetus.

I did quit my job as a vegetarian hash slinger and took temping jobs until I found a good fit working for a small local paper. The pay was poor but the boss, a woman in her sixties, looked like a possible mentor. She was fascinated by my life experience and wanted me to do a regular short column about it, along with handling ads. Doing the ads frightened me at first because it meant getting out in the community a lot, but I got into the groove and, for the first time in ages, started to feel proud of stretching my abilities.

I gave myself a "pause from men," but signs are clear that that won't be permanent. I vowed never to stray very far from the comfort of other females, and it wasn't long before this included joining the women's singing group I had avoided at first. Turns out they're all ages, sizes, colors, and singing ranges, and we all take care of each other.

When I raise my voice in Womansing, I'm not a wall-flower lost in the jungle of menopause. I'm proud of every cell in my body. I'm a sound blending with others, holding the secret of harmony in our hearts, letting it out little by little—together. 🦋

Grateful for My Body

by Stephanie Marston

ast summer, my doctor recommended that I have a bone scan to establish a base line to monitor bone loss as I went through menopause. When she called me with the results, we were both shocked. I had osteoporosis. I was incredulous. There must be some mistake. This kind of thing doesn't happen to me. I was sure that the young technician had miscalibrated the machine.

I called the imaging center and asked for a retest. As I lay on the table, tears rolled down my cheeks. I could see from the image on the machine that it matched the other scan. There was no mistake. I walked out to my car and burst into tears. Part of me wanted to pretend that this wasn't happening. It would be easy to do. I couldn't see it or feel it. I looked and felt fine, but I knew better. Denial would only seal my fate to end up as a frail old woman.

I had been healthy all my life. I mountain bike, do weight training, hike, and cross-country ski. I have a healthy diet. I've never smoked, and I don't drink carbonated beverages. I didn't fit the profile, but somehow, unbeknownst to me, termites were gnawing away at my bones, weakening my structure.

I began to question many of the things I was used to doing without a second thought. Could I still go cross-country skiing? What if I fell? What about hiking? Would I have to change my lifestyle? I found myself with a case of rampant paranoia. I bought a new pair of hiking boots with killer tread. I didn't want to fall. Suddenly the extra padding on my hips was a welcome cushion.

For the first time in my life, I felt as though my body had betrayed me. I felt as though I'd lost the body that had served me so well for all these years. I'd never been sick during my adult life. I had only gone to the doctor for routine exams or recently to cope with menopause. I was angry and scared. It wasn't that I had thought of myself as invincible, but I never imagined that I was going to face an illness, never mind this young. Now I was confronted with my own fragility. It just didn't fit my self-image. Suddenly I had fantasies of turning into a bog woman or ending up as a pile of dust. Not what I had imagined.

The osteoporosis forced me to change how I perceived myself and the world. While it was frightening at first, it was another instance of receiving a gift in black wrapping paper— you know, those lessons that come whether we want them or not. Not only was I being asked to let go of my image of myself as a young woman, I was learning to recognize how much we depend on our bodies remaining healthy. I began to listen to my body in a way I hadn't before. As Gloria Steinem put it, "Perhaps one of the rewards of aging is a less forgiving body that transmits its warnings faster—not as betrayal, but as wisdom." Our bodies demand that we shift our focus away from the frenzy of life toward a more mindful way of being. Now a woman can no longer deny the wisdom of her body.

Those of you who bore children might remember how during your pregnancy you were in closer touch with your bodily changes. Regardless of what we may have wanted to do, despite how much we may have wanted to feel that we were running the show, pregnancy taught us the lessons of surrender and attentiveness. We often had to cancel or reschedule plans in the face of our body's needs. In a similar way, we must now become attuned to our bodies.

If we treat our menopausal bodies with the same care and amazement that we treated our pregnant bodies, this phase of our lives would be understood for what it truly is—an invitation into the second half of our lives. Perhaps now as we go through this time of immense change, the same nurturing energy that we focused on the new life that was growing within our womb must now be refocused on giving birth to our newly emerging selves.

With menopause, we're compelled to surrender not only to our biology, but also to the inevitability of change itself, which can be daunting—if not frightening. Yet learning to accept the continuous process of change, each and every moment, is one of the central lessons offered by menopause. As we experience the change within our bodies, we become aware of our connection with something universal, something eternal. Menopause provides an opening for us to touch the sacred, the great mystery of life.

I recently had an experience that helped me to remember how vulnerable we are and the importance of being thankful for your body. I went to my regular Saturday morning yoga class. After some preliminary poses, the teacher had us kneel facing the wall with our pelvises touching it. She then instructed us to lean back, grab our ankles, and drop our heads into a backbend. I couldn't get near my heels. She noticed me struggling and came around behind me, placed her feet on my back, along my spine, and gently applied pressure as I reached around to grab her arms. Within seconds I was in tears. She took her feet away and asked if I was all right. I told her that her foot was pushing where I had broken my back twenty-three years ago. She reassured me, saying that backbends often release a lot of emotion. I felt a little embarrassed crying in a class with fifteen other people. I pulled myself together as best I could and did a modified version of the pose.

The instructor then demonstrated the next posture, which was very strenuous. I was certain that I wouldn't be able to do it. After a few failed attempts, the man lying next to me made a suggestion that he thought might help. I made the adjustment and was able to do the pose. I felt such a sense of triumph.

As we lay on the floor in a resting posture at the end of class, tears rolled down my cheeks. I realized how fortunate I am to not only be able to do yoga, but to walk, hike, ski—all the things I love that I take for granted. I felt myself fill with gratitude. I'm not confined to a wheelchair as doctors once expected. Here, despite the osteoporosis, I feel strong and capable. The feeling of gratitude stayed with me. I was filled with a sense of peace and well-being and an appreciation for the preciousness of life. ✎

Beyond the Madness

by Nancy Ilk

*I*n my early forties, I began to suspect something was going awry within my still-youthful-looking body. And typically, I blamed whatever weird, uncomfortable, or frightening symptom I was experiencing on my long-time companion: stress. Stress caused my heart to race; stress brought on sudden panic attacks; stress made me snap at my husband for no apparent reason other than he annoyed me just by breathing; stress made me feel as if I were slipping away from reality a little at a time; and it was stress that made me want to close my eyes and sleep forever. Stress. Not menopause. I was way too young for the "M" word. No one ever told me that menopause often slithers in early to groom you for the grand finale. Now that I'm in my fifties (and still waltzing with the hormones), I realize how sneaky and underhanded these hormones can be.

When I was forty-two, I packed up my two children, Jill, fifteen, and Brian, ten, and left my home of sixteen years. By home, I mean my comfortable bungalow, my husband, and two other grown daughters who still lived there. I had been married for twenty-three years at the time and knew if I didn't end my failed marriage, I would die. So, opting in favor of life, I set out on my own.

I found a small apartment not far from the old homestead and went about the business of creating a new life. My children and I managed fairly well on our own. I worked, took care of our apartment, and spent most of my spare time with the kids. I also cried a lot—not because I had regrets about my divorce but because I had regrets about my life in general. Throughout this time, I tried desperately to keep everybody happy, consoled, and secure. Sadly, though, I found that at this challenging and frightening time of my life, I had no family to console *me*.

But God works in mysterious ways. One day while walking out of a bank, I met my true Prince Charming. We married a year later. Skipping the honeymoon tradition altogether, we settled into married bliss immediately upon saying our "I do's." There was no time to waste. We had "families" to deal with. His and mine.

Somewhere during the next couple of years, my stress level began peaking. And peaking right along with it were my hormones. Subtle signs of perimenopause began appearing: mild flushes, increased anxiety, insomnia, mood swings (that was a biggie), paranoid thoughts (another biggie), fatigue (humongous!), heart palpitations, and various other telltale symptoms. I didn't know what they meant. I just assumed I was going nuts or dying. Or both.

As I approached my fiftieth year, I began experiencing even more hormone fluctuations. My mood "swings" now became "dives." At times, I went off the chart completely. I fought bouts of depression. I fought bouts of anxiety. I also had the misfortune to come down with irritable bowel syndrome (a nondelightful experience) and wound up in a hospital, where I was poked, prodded, and examined inside and out—literally. Severe stress, they said. Eat more fiber. Get more rest. Stop worrying. Chill. Ha!

Then, shortly after I turned the mystical age of fifty, old resentments and unresolved business concerning my three grown daughters surfaced. One daughter in particular, Sandy (the middle child, of course), had serious "issues" with me. To make a long story short, we talked—she walked. My other two daughters, being loyal siblings, followed, leaving me devastated.

During this painful time, I continued to struggle not only with family issues, but also with the frustrating and uncomfortable symptoms of menopause. Often, I felt sick, scared, and alone. All I had were books about menopause. And uninformed doctors.

And then, one day, while feeling hopeless and depressed, I sat at my computer and typed in the word "menopause." Up came several hits, one of them being a Web site called Power Surge. I clicked on it and began to read. I started crying as I read posts from women all over the world talking about the same things I was experiencing. Not just physical symptoms, but emotional ones as well. I read about their fears, their concerns, their triumphs, and their failures. I felt enormous relief when I realized that I wasn't alone! I wasn't some blubbering, horrible, idiotic menopausal woman who couldn't get her emotions under control. I was, to my great surprise, quite normal! I knew then that I had turned a corner in my life. I had found a place to go to when I needed reassurance and support. This new feeling of security had a profound and positive effect on how I began to define myself.

It was also around this time that I began to write. I started by journaling. Each morning (between flashes), I put pen to paper and wrote down my thoughts, fears, and frustrations. Amazingly, things in my life I had not acknowledged before now stared boldly back at me from the page; in between the lines, my authentic self began to emerge. Encouraged and excited, I decided to take my writing a step further: I began to write on the computer. I wrote poetry. I wrote short stories; I wrote essays; and I wrote my life story. I wrote through my fears and discomfort. Eventually, some of my work was published. No longer just a menopausal empty nester, I now had a purpose. A creative one.

If not for menopause knocking at my door and telling me to slow down and look within, I might not have stumbled onto this new path. Menopause is a change, not only chemically, but emotionally as well. It is a challenge. For me, menopause forced me to make some needed changes in my life. It taught me to take care of my body, mind, and spirit. It also taught me to put myself first, something I had rarely ever done before.

When I first began my experience with menopause, I didn't realize I was embarking on a journey. A journey that not only involved strange and oftentimes frightening physical symptoms, but a journey that would take me to a place I had never been before—inside myself. I discovered there's a whole lot more to me than what I present to the world; that I'm a pretty tough cookie when I need to be; that I'm more than a body, a face, and a personality; and that I am capable of *real* change. As a result of some of these changes, my relationships, as well as my life, are more meaningful. And although only two of my daughters have returned to the fold thus far, I am confident that all of us will be united one day soon.

We women are a hardy bunch. We endure an awful lot in this life. We bear silently most pains—physical and emotional. From the time we get our first period until the time we have our last, we weave bravely in and out of life's passages. It isn't an easy row to hoe, but all in all, we manage to do surprisingly well. No doubt about it—the woman's journey is a bumpy one, full of twists and turns, hormones and hysterics, laughter and tears. But with compassion, honesty, and a strong sense of humor on our part, we can beat the odds. That is, after all, what we do best. Hormones be damned! ❧

Blood, Toil, Tears, and Cats

by Rhonda Keith

On Labor Day weekend of 1997, I went to New York City with some friends for the International Yan Xin Qigong (pronounced "Yan Chin Chee Gung") Conference. I'd begun to practice the Yan Xin qigong method in Boston the preceding summer, and its effects were startling. For the first time in years I could sleep through the night, and a severe but unaccountable back pain vanished for good. When my son helped me move a houseful of furniture that summer, I noticed that I didn't get winded and seemed to have more strength and stamina, and my son observed that I was less irritable.

I was changing inside, too. Some changes were subtle, and even today I probably don't know everything that went on. But it was obvious that emotional and spiritual changes were occurring. I was calmer and happier, and people seemed to like me better. I liked them better too.

I was happy with what Dr. Yan Xin calls the highest body technology. So when I had the opportunity to join thousands of people from all over the world in New York for a conference where Dr. Yan Xin was to speak, I anticipated even more dramatic changes. I never could have guessed what form they would take. What I hoped for was generally improved health, more energy, even rejuvenation. I wasn't having much difficulty with the onset of menopause. It was merely annoying that one of the now less-regular periods had to start just when I was going out of town—a minor inconvenience for a four-hour road trip and a long weekend of seminars, lectures, and entertainment. But ever since I'd started menstruating at the age of eleven, when had it been convenient?

This was maybe only the third time I'd been in New York City, and I always love it. I shared a hotel room with some fascinating young Chinese women not far from Herald Square, a reasonable walk from the Jacob Javits Convention Center. Everyone had a story to tell about their qigong experiences, and the conference itself was terrific. Artists performed, and workshops covered the historical, scientific, philosophical, and personal aspects of the practice.

Aside from going to restaurants, I wouldn't have time to get around town, but when I rode into the city in a friend's car on Friday evening along the Hudson River, I saw something that made my heart lurch: the USS *Intrepid*. It had been heading for the scrap yard when it was rescued and turned into a museum docked in the Hudson. The *Intrepid* (nicknamed the "Mighty I" or the "Fighting I") is a CV-11, Essex class, 40,000-ton, 900-foot-long aircraft that launched in 1943 out of Norfolk, Virginia, heading for the South Pacific—with my father on board. Fresh off the farm, he'd joined the Navy in 1939. One day in 1944, the *Intrepid* took two kamikaze hits within five minutes and was barely able to limp back to San Francisco for repairs because of the huge hole in its side. A windbreak had to be made of what canvas they could collect on board, in order to steer the ship, and my dad probably helped make it. His job, still called "sailmaker," was to do the sewing for the ship. This included making flags into body bags for burials at sea.

When my dad died in 1990, I hadn't seen him for ten years, and we hadn't spoken for five. It doesn't matter now why; we'd driven each other apart for several reasons. My parents divorced painfully when I was fifteen, but the reasons were also generational, political, and philosophical, as well as personal. If I had a chance, I would do some things differently now, even if he wouldn't. But once or twice after he died, I'd felt him as a friendly unseen presence, although I wasn't looking for it or even consciously thinking about him. I had to visit his ship. So on a Saturday morning in 1997, I took two hours away from the qigong conference, walked the few blocks from the Javits Center, and bought my ticket.

A few old veterans volunteer their time as guides and docents on the museum ship, but there was little chance any of the vets had known my father from World War II; the ship carried at least 3,000 men. Only part of the carrier was open to the public in 1997, and there was no way of knowing where my dad would have worked and slept, but I knew that half a century earlier, he had crossed the same decks I did that day. A Japanese couple was touring the ship while I was there, with a father or grandfather who'd been a kamikaze pilot during the war—he had turned his plane back. He, too, had a past to reconcile. The ship was full of ghosts.

I saw as much as I could, bought a videotape about the ship, got the name of a veteran who had started a World War II *Intrepid* vets group back in Boston (which I later joined), and walked back to my conference, with no idea what was about to happen.

I believe it was no coincidence that I'd seen the *Intrepid* as I came into New York, but it wasn't until I returned to the conference that I felt something breaking loose in me. It was the ship, it was the qigong, it was me and my father. I couldn't stop crying, off and on, for the next three days, until I went back to Boston on Monday. And my period accelerated to a flood. I was crying top to bottom, for all that was lost and all that I wanted to say to my father and all that I wanted to hear from him. Maybe I was crying for him too, crying the tears he had difficulty letting loose.

I've always been a person who keeps a pretty tight grip on my emotions, most of the time. When I was about nineteen, I made myself stop weeping when I was sad, and since then seldom gave in to tears. Yet I knew my periods were sometimes affected by my emotions, and I couldn't control that. But this time I felt like I was simply a vessel, and the years of loss and sadness over my dad were being washed away by rivers of salt water and blood. I was in the ladies' room at least once an hour all weekend cleaning up the flow. It was hard to concentrate on what was going on around me at the conference, but I understood some things and trusted I was absorbing others by osmosis.

The only respite I had that weekend was during Dr. Yan Xin's four-hour talk on Monday. He spoke through a translator about qigong and about *de*—a Taoist terms that means, roughly, "virtue." Dr. Yan had trained with highly advanced Buddhist monks since he was four years old; he also has a Western medical degree. He says he emits qi energy, a Taoist concept of a kind of bio-energy, to the audience as he speaks. I listened for four hours, sitting up straight, not leaning back into the chair, in the qigong practice posture—and for four hours I did not have to go to the ladies' room to change my plugs and pads. But as soon as the lecture was over, the flood started again.

It continued when I went back to Boston and back to work, lasting an entire month. As someone once told me about herself in the same condition, I could have stood over a bucket. She had gotten a D&C; I chose to let it flow. As the weeks passed, however, I became more and more exhausted from the loss of blood. I couldn't do anything but go to work and go home and lie down. I asked one of my Chinese qigong friends about this phenomenon, and she said not to worry, it was a detoxification process. I believed her. My complexion began to look wonderful, as smooth and clear as a child's. Also, I had heard that my maternal grandmother had bled heavily during menopause. She had just put up with it till it ended, so I was ready to believe it was a natural process, and I wasn't afraid. But after a few weeks I decided to go to my local Chinese herbalist, who gave me an herbal tea that stopped the bleeding. One Chinese doctor had started it; one stopped it.

Beyond the physical aspect of this phenomenon, I felt that the purging had something to do with getting rid of the years of bitterness, certainly toxic, stemming from my broken relationship with my dad, so I was willing to endure. Sometimes I wonder what would have happened if I'd let it continue. Did I give up too soon? Did I need more purification? As a feminist, I reject the idea that menstruation is a "purification" because that implies the body is unclean. However, as a woman, I know that my body has often given expression to pains that my mind rejected—cysts in the breast, menstrual fluctuations, shrinking and expansion of body parts, enforced rest due to exhaustion. The body suffers, diagnoses, and cures.

And certainly menstruation ushers in a new beginning of sorts every month.

Since that weekend in New York, I feel as if my father and I reconciled in spirit. The qigong was both a catalyst and a healer, and I think the hormonal hoo-hah happened just to make sure my attention didn't wander from what was really going on: a spiritual work, forgiveness, letting go, peace.

My last period went from 2001 to 2002. I hadn't had a period for about a year, but I started bleeding just before I was to drive from Boston to Ohio for Christmas—yep, another road trip, a longer one this time, and in winter. What a drag. Then I got an unexpected e-mail from a man I hadn't seen or heard from for more than twenty-five years. We were good friends, but though I'd cared about him deeply, he'd faded out of my life: just one more loss. Now he'd tracked me down via the Internet. It wasn't easy. It took a few miracles to make this reconnection happen. He was still living in Ohio, and we made plans to meet the day after New Year's Day.

We talked nonstop for two days. At one point, my eyes filled with tears as I was talking about something, though I didn't want to cry, and he told me later that my tears touched his heart. We returned to our homes, and between us wrote a book via e-mail over two months.

Once again, I didn't stop bleeding for a solid month. I felt as if something inside me must have known he was coming. It was important, and this time we wouldn't drift apart—if I could let something loose inside. And that's what happened. We got engaged, and I moved to Ohio. I haven't bled since. Tears will rise from time to time, but not as often as laughter.

You never know until later which is your last period, but I think the one in 2002 was my last. For more than forty years, my body was a commentator, a predictor and analyst, a witness to my internal life. Now it's changed, and I can't rely on my hormones to nudge me when my understanding leaves off. And maybe menstruation really is a purification, releasing toxins that build up around the complex emotional and sexual lives most women have. I wish I had thought of that all those years—more than four decades—when I was cramping, tired, and generally annoyed by the inconvenience.

I remind myself of a pleasant gray cat I used to have who delivered a few litters of kittens before I had her fixed. After a couple of cycles, I noticed something odd about her. When her hormones were in full spate, she was a vivid presence with a kind of alert tension, but when she wasn't in heat, pregnant, or nursing, she had an insubstantial air about her, like a ghost ship drifting around the house, or a grayed-out computer screen icon that you can't click on. It was as if reproduction made her real, or clear. However, after I had her spayed, she became solidly herself again, all the time. Maybe that is happening to me. I've always had a life other than the reproductive—education, work, travel—but now I'm no longer slowed by menstruation, fidgety from lust, glowing with pregnancy, or contentedly maternal. Maybe I am becoming more solidly myself.

Love—Finally!

by Sally Kaplan

t age forty-five, never married, I had certainly had my
share of dating and relationship experiences. But nothing
could have prepared me for the incident I am about to recount.

Bill and I first met at a party. He was a guest at the dinner I
was videotaping for a food show I am producing as a television
pilot. My attraction to him was so immediate, I couldn't bear
to stand near him—my breath would quicken and my heart
would palpitate. The attraction wasn't merely physical, though
he *is* a striking man—in his early fifties, with a wash of white
hair and a smile to die for. No, the attraction was far more
overwhelming. It was pregnant with all that "could be"
between myself and this new man—as if a full-length story
about to take place might begin this very night. Thank God I
was working that night as a director of a television shoot. It
gave me a good excuse to stay focused on what I was doing
and, to the best of my capacity, ignore him.

At one point, I remember hiding behind my cameraman's
shoulder, pretending to look at the scene in front of us in the
kitchen. Bill was seated behind me at the long dinner table and
I distinctly remember the feeling of his eyes on me—curious,

flirtatious, sexy. A moment later, Bill approached me from behind and offered a suggestion on what shot to get, and I nearly fainted from the magnetism of my attraction—his low sexy voice whispering in my ear to frame the steam coming off the pasta just so. And I knew it. I was hooked.

When the evening was over, as I was driving home to the simple bungalow where I was housesitting for a friend of a friend in Venice Beach, I couldn't stop thinking about Bill. The inner cinema that was running inside my head kept repeating the tiny moments he and I had shared that night—the nuances that shadowed a stare, a glance, a smile. When I lay down to go to sleep that night in that borrowed bed, self-doubt invaded the pressure of my fantasy. I counted all the reasons why he would never want to be with me. He was too good-looking; he was too successful; he was probably married; or better yet, he was gay.

In a situation like this, what is a woman to do? Especially a woman who was so gun-shy from so many love affairs that hadn't worked out and from so many disastrous dates? Well, the very next day, my friends did it for me. Three people from the dinner party called me and said, "Sally, you have to call this guy. He can help you. He works in the industry as a director, he knows reality-TV people, he can help you find work or an editor or something. If you want to stay in L.A., you should call him. Just call him!"

"This could be easy," I thought. I could call him about work. And at least we could talk again, or meet again, or rub up against each other again or whisper into each other's ears or *something!* So I did. I called him and left a message on his machine. I kept it very business-like: "Glad to have met you briefly last night. Don and Craig and Karen suggested I contact you because we work in the same field and I wondered if I could take you out for a coffee or a beer or something and pick your brain about editors, work in reality television, blah blah blah."

Within a few hours I heard back from Bill. "I'd be delighted," he said. Little did I know that he had already called Don and Craig and Karen in order to ask them about me. He wanted to meet me at Musso and Frank's, which happens to be one of my favorite restaurants in Los Angeles, but it was closed on Mondays. So off we went to the Pig and Whistle at 5:00 that afternoon. We did talk about work. But that was not all. In fact, we spent two hours talking about everything under the sun, from politics to weather to hiking to producing to good food to the history of L.A. to Colorado and more. We also shared a Caesar salad and a plate of fried calamari, which I was so glad he had ordered because it was my favorite thing on the menu, too. I insisted on paying (it was a work meeting, after all) and then he insisted on walking me to my car (it was a tougher part of Hollywood). We stood for a moment in front of my car and shared that awkward "goodbye" moment, and I wondered to myself how or if we would see each other again. Bill broke the silence with, "Would you like to take a hike with me next time? I can show you some favorite haunts."

"I am more or less a 'long stroll' person than a hiking person, but yes," I said. "I would like that," and we said goodbye.

That night I had trouble going to sleep. I was faced with a dilemma I didn't know how to solve. Although I was a product of the '60s and feminism, I wanted to sit back and wait for *him* to make the next move. I wanted to be the princess or lady, actively pursued by the prince or gentleman. But I was aware that if that was what I truly wanted, how could he know it?

The next morning I e-mailed Bill. I thanked him for taking the time with me and added that aside from all the help he offered me in the work realm, I also enjoyed meeting with him because he seemed like such a wonderful person. Thank God for e-mail. It makes even a shy person feel bold.

Bill invited me to go for a walk the next week, and I agreed to meet him at Don's house. Unfortunately, it was raining, so Bill suggested we go to an adorable local family-style Mexican restaurant where all the women wore colorful Mariachi singer outfits. Afterward, we spent a long time sitting in Bill's parked car talking about everything—the fact that he had two girls and I had no children; that he had been married twice and I had never married; and that he had not really successfully dated anyone for the last five years because his children came first and it took a woman with a very strong constitution not to take that personally.

I described my tendency to attract depressive-type men, and he told me about his tendency to attract crazy women. Though an appropriate pause declared itself, we never kissed. I just lowered my glance, thanked him, and said goodnight. Even on that drive home, though I knew this was the man for me, I had no idea how he felt. I just didn't know what to do next.

So I did nothing.

"In romance, timing is everything," my grandmother always said. Suffice it to say, the timing wasn't right. Bill left for Vermont to do some research for a film, and I went back to Boulder, Colorado, to try to re-sublet my apartment. I was only living in Los Angeles for a few months to "try it out" before moving there permanently. The best Bill and I could do over the next few weeks was stay in touch via a couple of e-mails.

When Bill and I both finally returned to Los Angeles, he called me. "I would like to take you out on a date," he said. "I mean a *real* date."

"Well, isn't that sort of what we did last time, I mean when we went out for dinner?"

"Not really," he said. "I mean I would like to take you out on a real date, you know like when I come to pick you up at your house, and I take you to a really nice place for dinner and we have a really nice time and then I pay for it and then I take you home. You know, more like that."

A true prince, in a fifty-year-old handsome body! I loved it. "Okay, then," I said. "I would like that."

A *real date.*

He drove all the way from Highland Park to Venice Beach to pick me up. I was all dressed up and quite nervous when I answered the door. He was sweaty and clearly tired from the one-and-a-half hours he had been sitting in traffic to get to me. He drove me to James Beach, a lovely restaurant frequented by independent filmmaker types in Venice. The valet parked the car, and we proceeded inside. Though it was a quite cool March night, we agreed to sit outside on the patio. After all, there were plenty of heat lamps.

Bill led me to the table. We sat down, he ordered Chardonnay and oysters, and we started talking. Well I should say, *he* started talking. And talking. And talking. For reasons I did not understand, I was actually finding it quite hard to listen to a word he was saying. Something else was taking over me—something I had never experienced before. A wave of heat and dizziness entered my body and crawled up inside me like a monster that needed to get out. I felt like I was about to faint. If I had a zipper on my skin like a wet suit, I would have wanted to unzip it and crawl out of it right then and there. I would have preferred to stand naked on the table of a trendy Los Angeles restaurant than experience that infernal heat. But Bill kept talking as if nothing were happening. At first I tried to suppress the violence of all that was bubbling up inside me. Then I tried to find the strength to excuse myself and go to the ladies' room or outside to catch my breath, but it was too late. I was leaning forward, acting as if I was listening to this very interesting conversation, and sweat started pouring down my face. All I could think about was, "Here I am on my first 'real date' with a man I really like, and I have just fallen off the boat. Help!" I thought, as I tried to ground myself so as not to faint. Finally, he stopped talking and took me in.

"Are you all right?" Bill asked.

A voice from deep inside me unleashed a high, curdled scream, *"No, I am not all right!"*

The poor guy receded into the leather cushion of his booth chair. If I could have read his mind, he would have been saying to himself, "Oh no, here I go again, another crazy woman, all I need." Instead, he asked sincerely, "What's wrong?"

I continued, still screaming at the top of my lungs: "Bill, you have to get them to turn the heat lamp off *now*. I am dying or something, and if it is all right with you I think I need to take my shirt off because I think I am going to faint. Thank God I have a camisole on underneath! What is happening to me? Do you think it is a hot flash or something?"

Without blinking, he completely switched gears, from "I barely know this crazy woman and I don't know what to do" to being the director of a dramatic scene in a multimillion-dollar movie. Simultaneously, he hollered for the waiter to come over and instructed me to move over to the corner of the booth for a minute. I obeyed him. He was, after all, the only thing grounding me. I crawled into the corner of the booth and asked him, "Why am I over here?"

He answered, "To get away from the heat lamp. Waiter!"

When the waiter came over, this time it was Bill who screamed, "Turn the heat lamp off *now*." The young man looked at him, frightened, and said, "But *signor,* I am so sorry, but if I were to turn off the lamp above your table I would have to turn the heat off in the entire restaurant and it is cold tonight, *signor.*"

Bill did not even give the guy a glance. Instead, he boomed, "Then turn the heat off in the whole restaurant. *Now.*"

The waiter departed. By now, the entire trendy restaurant had eyes on us as I continued to hover in my corner until the heat lamp went off on top of our table, and throughout the restaurant. I took a deep breath and repositioned myself back in my spot in the center of the booth. The sweat began to evaporate from my cheeks. I cleared my throat. Ate an oyster. Tasted my wine. And Bill never mentioned what had happened again that whole evening.

Bill drove me home, kissed me on the cheek, and said goodnight.

I went inside and got into bed. On top of the covers (still too overheated to get under them), I took a deep breath and said to myself, "If I never hear from this guy again for the rest of my life, I would understand. How could he be with someone like me?"

And I fell asleep.

The next morning, I called my mother. Like a thirteen-year-old talking about her first period, I told her about my first hot flash and my date. I also told her I would not be surprised if I never heard from the guy again. In her Bronx New York Jewish accent, she replied, "Honey, you are right, you may never hear from this guy again. But if you do, I mean if he does get back in touch with you after all that, you know what? This guy is a keeper."

Bill e-mailed me that morning to say how lovely it had been to see me and how much he enjoyed our dinner. He invited me to join him at his house a few days later. He had some close friends he wanted me to meet. He never mentioned "the incident" at James Beach.

Bill was a keeper all right.

Bill and I have been together now for over two years. We are talking about the possibility of sharing a home together. He treats me like a queen more than a princess. I treat him like the prince or king he deserves to be. He says he is crazy about me and that he waited twenty-five years for me to show up. I tell him how in love I am with him and how lucky I am to have met him.

Sometimes in the middle of the night I throw the covers off in a heap and it wakes Bill up. He leans over to me and whispers into my ear, "What's the matter, honey? You having a hot flash or something?" And I say, "Shhhhhhh." And we try to go back to sleep. When I am just too hot to fall back asleep, Bill sings me a song he made up called "Hot Flash Sally." He reminds me, "Women don't have hot flashes, they just have power surges."

I squish the pillow under my head, stare at the moonlight beaming through the venetian blinds of his bedroom window and sigh to myself in domestic bliss: "So this is what happens when you fall in love at middle age . . ." ❧

three

The Meditative Journey

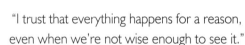

"I trust that everything happens for a reason,
even when we're not wise enough to see it."

~ Oprah Winfrey

Mirror, Mirror

by Madeena Spray Nolan with Amy Lynch

I swore off makeup on my twenty-fifth birthday. That day, as I looked searchingly in the mirror, it hit me that the better I got at applying makeup from then on, the bigger the shock would be when I took it off. For years after that, I had a friendly, if distant, relationship with the mirror. I looked in it to see that I had myself together. All in all, I was pleased with what I saw. That changed when I turned fifty. Now I find myself looking longer. And what do I see? New lines, drying skin, and, on some mornings, circles around my eyes. Yet my mirror still reassures me; I look into my eyes and see the same person I always was. But photographs are something else again. They utterly betray. That person with short gray hair around a jowly face. Who is that?

• • •

I know the psychic split I'm describing sounds a little crazy; it feels like it, too. How can I thoroughly like my face in my morning mirror but be completely disconcerted by the way I look in photos? How can I walk out my front door carrying with me two distinctly different notions of how I look to the world, never knowing which one will show up when I glimpse myself while passing a store window?

At least I'm not alone here. In her landmark study of midlife women, psychologist Terri Apter discovered that most of us go through some weirdness regarding our appearance during our forties and fifties. The mirror shows us somebody we're not used to being, a likeness that seems to disguise rather than reveal us. As a result, at one time or another, most of us develop a dizzying split vision. On one hand, we "see" ourselves from the inside out ("Oh yes, that devastatingly vibrant and attractive person is me!") and, at the same time, we're unsettled by how people may think we look. When Peggy Orenstein surveyed women coast-to-coast for her book *Flux: Women on Sex, Work, Love, Kids and Life in a Half-Changed World,* she found that during our forties, whether single or married, mothers or not, women look into the mirror and recognize the internal self as different from the one in the glass. In other words, there's me, and then there's *me.*

Doris Lessing called this the "great secret" of midlife. "Your body changes," she wrote, "but you don't change at all. And that of course causes great confusion." Can't decide if you're luscious or a frump? Join the club. Fortunately, psychologists say this is a normal sign of growth, a step toward taking charge of your life, including your image, in a new way. Here's hoping, because just about the same time we're feeling schizo about how we look to the world, it gets worse. The world stops seeing us at all.

• • •

My friend Ronna, forty-eight, is a willowy redhead who has always attracted attention. But recently she told me about sitting in a doctor's waiting room when two men entered and didn't look at her at all. Not a glance. Out of habit, Ronna had been poised to receive the usual acknowledgment of her good looks. When it didn't come, she was without a script. "I knew what to do if they noticed me, but not what to do if they didn't," she said. It hits all of us at one time or another. Suddenly or slowly, we are no longer on the radar screen of people, especially men, we encounter. Maybe they look at younger women instead. Maybe they look at our daughters. *Ouch*. This is a *loss*. Loss of power, loss of the youthful attractiveness that once came to us so easily. We look better, healthier, younger, more appealing, than women of earlier generations. Naturally, we want to hold on to that for as long as we can. But like it or not—and who does?—feeling invisible is normal, too. In fact, psychologists argue that once we experience invisibility, we can break free of the "outside eye" that causes our split vision. We reclaim our own faces and bodies and feel stronger for it. But don't get me wrong. Nobody says that's easy.

• • •

You can tell something about where you are in this process by the way you look into your mirror. Apter observed that the forty-something women approach the mirror by glancing lower than their eyes, somewhere close to chin level. No, not because our chins are sagging! Rather, we tend to protect ourselves from an overall view of our faces. This is a signal of that split image we talked about earlier. But fifty-something women approach their faces differently. At that age, we meet our eyes in the mirror often and are more comfortable with a spontaneous, admiring sweep of the entire image. Eventually, we re-envision ourselves as "older" without finding that a flaw.

In her research, Orenstein identified the emergence of voice as part of this process. She found midlife women feeling invisible to others at the very same time that they were working to become more visible internally to themselves. They were speaking up more often, gaining more authentic voices. Power of appearance might have been declining, but power of personality was growing. I know that's true for me. At fifty-eight, I speak out in groups where I used to remain silent, and when I do, the people around me, including those who have stopped looking at me, listen. More and more, I don't need a mirror to feel pleased with myself.

· · ·

You may reclaim your image early or late during midlife, and you may do it more than once. And if you get stuck in double vision at some point, unhappy with the mirror and wanting only to turn back the clock, that's understandable. At times like that, it's easy just to rush right in and fix what's falling. In a world where youth and power are so closely aligned, and during a time when we don't yet have many models for how to claim power as we age, the question of whether or not to have aesthetic procedures is complex and individual. The dilemma is this: Will the facelift, tummy tuck, or Botox hold you back from doing the vital work of re-envisioning yourself as a woman come of age, a woman of experience and power? Or will it increase your confidence and help you align the inner and outer view of yourself? *Stilling* is key here, stopping to ask, "Is this about how I choose to see myself, or is it about how the world sees me?" It's a complicated task, laying claim to this very personal thing, the image that is "me" to each of us.

In the end, there is comfort in knowing that confusion is a normal part of working through this puzzle. Comfort in finding that year after year, we understand more deeply that each of us is more layered and interesting than a mirror or photo can ever capture.

Maybe that's why psychologists report that the measures of beauty we develop during midlife are broader and gentler than those we use when we are young. Ultimately, we become more apt to recognize loveliness in all kinds of different faces. Starting with our own. 🐝

Reprinted with permission from Ourselves.com. *Ourselves: Women at the Center of Life* is a newsletter for women who are changing. Articles cover transitions, dealing with stress, money, work, and new ideas. Subscribe at *www.ourselves.com*.

Word by Word

by Anne Lamott

I had this beautiful feminist friend named Nora, who once said, "I've been thinking about killing myself, but I want to lose five pounds first." I was remembering this recently, because I started liking this guy. He liked me back but was just getting out of a relationship with a young woman. *Young* young—he showed me her picture one day, and she was tall, coltish, alive, thin, raven-haired. Right around this time when I was first starting to think about this guy in the biblical sense, I was at my most incredibly unyoung. I was tired, jet-lagged, stressed to the nu-nus, loggy after three weeks of fatty petroleum-product food. Sort of like a dreadlocked cross between Richard Jewell and Rose Kennedy. Of course, I told myself, there is beauty in being older, being a mother, there is the beauty of letting go of a lot over the years, there is beauty in the wise steady gaze. But I kept thinking of this young woman and how beautiful she was and how un—what is the word—dilapidated. Later that same day, I went to a mirror and looked for a long time and tried to see the timeless glory of crow's feet, the resplendence of having survived, the beauty of tired green eyes.

What I saw instead is a woman who is forty-two on the outside, who grew up playing all day in the sun. And that shows up in my skin. But who knew? Then I had just a few thousand too many social drinks; and then I became a single mother. And the long and short of it is that I look like a fabulous woman who is on sale at the consignment store.

I am trying to accept that I am no longer in extremely late youth, as I like to tell myself. That actually I'm m-m-m-m-m-middle-aged. And even though I am a feminist and even though I am religious, I secretly believe in some mean little rat part of my brain, that despite those beliefs, I *am* my skin, my hair, and, worst of all, those little triangles of fat that pouch at the top of the thighs that we call Brooklyns around here. In other words, that I am my packaging. Even though both paths teach me that I am the person inside, the spirit, the heart, all that I have survived, all that I have given over the years, after I started liking this guy, a funny thing happened: I looked in the mirror, and sighed, and forgot all about that, and thought to myself, I will cut my eyes out.

But in the same mirror I saw a framed prayer on the wall, from when Sam was four, and we were at a friend's house for dinner late one summer day after we had been lost for hours. And at the dinner table, my boy Sam who was hot and sweaty and hungry somehow managed to get his head caught in the slats of his chair; no one noticed for a moment, until, in this tiny Tweety-Bird voice, Sam was heard saying, "I need help with me."

I thought it might be the best prayer I ever heard. I said it out loud the day I decided to cut my eyes out: I need help with me.

Ten minutes later some friends called and invited me to a movie about gypsies, a documentary called *Latcho Drom,* which means "safe passage." I really had no interest in seeing it. What I really wanted to do right then was to go watch *First Wives Club* and see all these extremely rich actresses who had had face-lifts and breast implants and dermabrasion and collagen and who have personal trainers. What I really wanted to do was to go see a little revenge, because I was scared already about liking this guy. But okay, gypsies, I said to my friends.

I sat there in the dark waiting for the gypsy movie to begin, staring at the blank screen as if it were a graven image, thinking bitter thoughts. From time to time I tugged on the skin of my upper eyelid, which I can now pull out about two inches, like one of those old roll-up shades. I ate a four-ounce Kit Kat bar in an attempt to console myself, and by butt instantly began to feel like a beanbag chair.

And then the movie began.

They are all born old, the gypsies. The men are so dashingly homely, as if cars have ridden over their faces. The young girls are beautiful beyond words; and the oldest women dance. But the middle-aged mothers looked just like me and my friends, tired, baggy, in some need of repair. Their faces are so exhausted with what it has taken to raise children on the tightrope walk of gypsy life; because when you're on the high wire, you have to use every bit of grace and skill and awareness and loyalty just to get to the other side. That's the gift, to have to use that kind of attention, that focus; and it shows up around your eyes.

The film also showed that for the gypsies, as with all nomads, if you don't keep walking, you die, so you figure out how to keep walking. That effort to keep moving shows on the mothers' faces, the exhaustion of exposure, of making sure both that the old people keep moving and that the babies are carried safely. The mothers, women in the last gasps of carnality, are the sandwich women, like us, taking care of their own mothers, taking care of the young.

But oh, the old women dancing: the old women who shine with the incredible stirring of spirit that kept them lit over the years, even though the winds are howling all around them. It's so different from when old women dance at our parties, and people nudge each other with their elbows because it's sort of cute and horrifying at the same time, like having the dead or hidden insist on stepping out onto the dance floor, Isak Dinesen attempting the Macarena. But the crowd of gypsies, outside in winter, huddled together at train stations, squatters and outlaws, cold, exposed, stand around while the music begins to play, and the old women seem to cackle, "Oh what the hell," and they start dancing. They've stopped chasing anything down, and you feel the rush of life force that this frees up inside them. Their gnarled witchy fingers are on the carotid artery of the culture, the link between the living and the dead, and in their faces and their bodies and their movement, you see the beauty of having come through.

The younger gypsies think the old ones are beautiful—watching this movie, you absolutely know that to be true. They think they're beautiful, like Isabella Rossellini or Liv Tyler. These old women sing in their scratchy crone voices of bottomless sadness, and yet they dance. They stuff so much into themselves, food stolen and shared, passion, care, to keep the system alive, to keep the whole thing burning like potbellied stoves. And they do, they burn.

It's so sexy and intimate and stark that you almost have to look away. Watching them most attentively, of course, are children, the girl children. There's a beautiful girl in the movie, beautiful like Anne Frank, who looks about twelve—but from another century, like all the gypsies look, taking the stuff of our nightmares and dreams, and living right on the edge of that, of all that we protect ourselves from. She's at the back of a very plain tavern, with her much younger brother, and the two of them are watching the men drink. There seems to be only drink and music, no food—I suppose because the room is neat, with a roughhewn cleanness, and food is messy. Or else they are too poor for the food. So the men play and sing and drink, and at first the girl watches. The tavern is someplace where no one else wants to be, where all these people who've snuck through the system can sit and drink and dance. There are only men inside, though, and this girl and her much younger brother. It's one family, though, that gypsy family, of people who have been told for centuries, "You're messy, you're dirty, dangerous, and you're not part of our family." So of course the sense of extended family is so fierce, and the girl is watching the men of her family dance in the front of the tavern. The young brother is very solemn, tentative, like he is worried that they're going to be discovered and asked to leave, but the girl watches, knowing, dark and dirty, smiling, shy. There is such a purity in her face as she watches the men; and then she begins dancing. She's practicing. A sense of grace and mastery comes out of her, like a strong shiny shoot, because she's paying such attention and she knows the shoot is going to flower. And she is going to dance, dance hungry, dance full, dance each cold astonishing moment, now, when she is young, and again, when she is old.

But if the fortune of the girl is the newness, is being the bud, and the fortune of the crone is in the freedom, the lack of clinging, where does that leave a youngish middle-aged

American woman like me? Maybe it leaves me needing to consider the extraordinary wealth of knowing that the girl of my past is still in me, and a marvelous dreadlocked crone is in the future; that I hold both of these females inside.

You know what I realized coming out of that movie that day? That I want what the crones have. Time for all those long deep breaths, time to watch more closely, time to learn to enjoy what I've always been afraid of—the sag and the invisibility, the ease of understanding that life is not about doing. That that was all a lie. Because the crones know this, and it gives them all kinds of time, time to get much much much less done, time for all these holy moments.

So I've been thinking about this guy I sort of like, and how, realistically, I am probably not going to lose five pounds before I see him next, or have the little canopy above my eyes snipped off. And how, spiritually speaking, I think what I am going to do instead is to begin practicing cronehood as soon as possible: to breathe, watch, smile, crookedly, dance. 🦋

Fearing, Facing, and (Finally!) Embracing Forty

by Sandy Henry

he clock struck twelve. I stood at the mirror, dimly lit by the full moon streaming through the window. I leaned in, searching my reflection. After about thirty seconds of sameness, I exhaled. It was finally here. I was forty.

I lumbered back to bed—I was now of legal lumbering age. I groaned. My husband, just a few months into his fortieth year, slept soundly. He was oblivious to my anxiety. Did he not realize that I was old—literally twice the age I had been when we met? No, he was clueless.

I lay on my back, thinking about all the things I was now too old to do, wear, be. I guess a tattoo was out, I thought. As if I'd ever seriously entertained the idea of inflicting that kind of pain on myself anyway. Who did I think I was? Cher? Maybe she had the tush to pull off a tattoo in middle age, but even at my youngest, fittest, firmest best, I was no Cher.

I looked at my nails in the semi-darkness. I needed a manicure. French, with stark white tips. No more cobalt blue. Glow-in-the-dark was history. And glitter? Positively silly at "my age."

I couldn't sleep. The anticipation of turning forty, which had begun on my thirty-ninth birthday, had nagged at me all day, and I had actually forgotten to eat dinner. That was a first. In all my thirty-nine, er, *forty* years, I had never before forgotten to eat.

I shuffled to the kitchen (shuffling is slower than lumbering, for those keeping score). I opened the fridge and grabbed the milk. Skim. Huh. At my age, I needed all the calcium I could get, so maybe I should at least switch to 1 percent. Better write that down before I forget.

I grabbed the Cap'n Crunch from the top shelf of the cupboard. Hmmm. That's a kids' cereal, and I was, after all, no kid. Better buy some bran flakes, or better yet, oat bran. I could pick that up on my next trip to the market, along with a copy of *Modern Maturity.*

I poured the skim milk over the crunchy yellow squares. I would miss Cap'n Crunch. And Kraft Mac and Cheese. But I wouldn't miss the skim milk.

I crunched on the cereal, the sharp, not-yet-soggy edges cutting into my gums. How long would I have my own teeth, I wondered? Both my parents had died with dentures. Funny, I never thought to ask how old they were when they had gotten them. They were probably forty.

I sat down with some warm milk and my old scrapbook. I paged through photos, programs, ticket stubs, a virtual log of my youth. There was an ancient picture of Mike Gillis and me on my very first date. I was fourteen, and I had primped all day—apple shampoo, melon scrub, cherry lip-gloss. I smelled like a freaking fruit salad. Funny that I could still remember that. And for one brief moment, I didn't feel forty.

Then there was a program from my high school graduation. Good God. I was actually old enough to be a parent to an eighteen-year-old. And I thought that it is probably a bit more confusing to age when you're not known as "Kayla and Connor's mom." Somehow, I would guess, having children would likely force one to be (or at least feign being) a mature individual.

I plucked another memory from the album, a dog-eared picture of a group of us at a screening of *The Rocky Horror Picture Show*. We were right out of high school, and we all worked together at a local movie theater. This frequent weekend activity, at eighteen, was harmless fun. We tried it again a dozen years later, and believe me when I say it is no longer amusing to be nailed in the head by a flying frozen "Frankenfurter" at thirty. At forty, it could be lethal.

I glanced at the clock. It was after 1 A.M. and I had to be up for work in the morning. That was definitely another thing I was much too old for—staying up late and getting up early.

The warm milk wasn't cutting it. I wanted a real drink. But I couldn't overdo it. I had to get up early, after all. And getting stupid drunk, though amusing to the drunk at nearly any age, is generally not so funny to anyone else. Actually, it could be sad. And although I was nearly catatonic about my advancing age, I wasn't really sad. What was sad, I thought, was the memory of those in my life who didn't make it to forty. My cousin Michelle had died of pancreatitis just weeks shy of her thirty-ninth birthday. A former friend and colleague had been killed by a stalker when she was barely thirty-five.

And Princess Diana, familiar and beloved to people the world over, had perished so young. Yes, I thought as I sipped my white wine. I had much to be grateful for, and forty wasn't looking so bad.

And on the subject of looks, many women over forty look incredible. Take Demi Moore, for example. She had just appeared on magazine covers in a bikini, touting her upcoming role in the sequel to *Charlie's Angels*. And she looked fabulous at forty. Or Morgan Fairchild, whose Old Navy Commercial was playing softly on my television screen as I paged through my memories. Cripe, she must be fifty at least, and she was probably still getting carded in bars. I took a gulp, picturing Morgan and Demi in my mind. Another drink couldn't hurt, I thought. And perhaps those two were bad examples. After all, everybody knows they're not from this planet.

But I could drink a toast to a number of other positive female role models whom I admired. All of my favorite actresses—Joanne Woodward, Kathy Bates, Susan Sullivan—were still vital, healthy, working. And they had all hit their stride in their forties and beyond. My favorite writers, Joy Fielding and Ann Rule, were topping the bestseller lists without missing a beat.

And the wonderful women in my own life are amazing yardsticks by which to measure a full and satisfying existence. My mother-in-law, who is in her sixties, still has the softest, most beautiful skin I've ever seen. And her mother, now ninety-one, lives on her own, cooks her own meals, and gets around better than most people half her age.

There's my favorite aunt, Rita, who, at nearly seventy, is enjoying what can only be called an active retirement. Along with my Uncle Joe, she travels frequently, spends time with her children and grandchildren, and plays a mean eighteen holes. And she looks virtually the same as she did when I was, ahem, young.

Then there's my new friend, Janet. She raised two children, including her son who is hearing-impaired, on her own. And now that same son is in medical school. And there is nothing about that woman that shows any trace of her fifty years.

I sipped the last of my wine and checked the clock. It was nearly 2:30 in the morning. And I was still forty. But surprisingly, I wasn't tired. Perhaps now was a good time to give myself that much-needed manicure.

I awoke before the alarm, a little past six. The room was still dark, but the sun struggled to poke through the window. And strangely, nothing seemed changed. My husband greeted me with a "Happy birthday" and a quick kiss. Then he squinted up his eyes and took my fingers in his. "Nice color," he muttered sleepily, no doubt admiring my blue, glow-in-the-dark glitter nail polish. 🖎

Today's Grandma

by Jozette Aaron

"Does your grandma have gray hair too?" I asked my best friend, Jessica, as we sat side by side on the stoop of her apartment building, enjoying a lazy summer afternoon. It was 1958 and I was eleven years old.

"I don't know . . . never met my grandma, but my mom has gray hair and she's a grandma . . . does that count?" Jessica asked hopefully.

"I guess . . . Do *all* grandmas have gray hair?" I continued, occupied now with removing a scab from my knee, head bent to the task as I dug stubby, bitten-off fingernails into the edges, wincing when I hit a raw spot not yet healed.

"Yes . . . they have to, otherwise they wouldn't be grandmas—right? And they have lots of wrinkles too. If wonder if they have to knit . . . 'cause my mom knits, and she's a grandma," Jessica announced, wanting so badly to have her mom fit the profile of what we believed grandmothers to look like.

"I don't think so. My grandma doesn't knit, but she's still my grandma. She has lot o' wrinkles, though, so I guess it's okay if she doesn't," I stated as I loosened the dried skin and flicked it off of my knee.

Even on television, a grandmother was portrayed as a woman who was short, pleasingly plump, with gray hair worn up in a respectable bun. She wore a housedress, usually in a tiny floral print, with an apron tied around her ample waist to keep the dress clean. She baked cookies—lots of them—and her house was always spotless, leaving her more time to sit in her rocker, watch the Lawrence Welk show, and knit a pair of socks, mittens, or a hat that would make a Christmas present for one of her many grandchildren. This is the image I grew up associating the title "grandmother" with.

Mom called me in for dinner just as I was about to relay this vital information to my pal, so Jessica and I had to cut this all-revealing conversation short. We stood up, dusted our bottoms off to keep from "dragging dirt into the house," as Mom always called it, and went our separate ways promising to finish the discussion another time.

When I got inside, I asked my mother if "grandma always had gray hair and wrinkles?"

"No, she had blond hair when I was a child, but it went gray and she doesn't dye it so I guess, to you, it would seem that way," Mom said, a smile tugging at the corners of her mouth. "Why do you ask?"

"Oh nothing . . . I was just wondering that's all." I responded . . . a triumphant smile shaping my lips. "*I knew it! I knew I was right . . . all grandmas do have gray hair!*" I said to myself as I set the table for dinner. "*Wait til I tell Jess.*"

Jessica and I never *did* get back to that conversation, but it stayed with me for a long time. Each visit to my grandma's made me more determined never to look like that when I'm a grandma . . . never! I loved my grandmother dearly and to me, since that was the only way she has looked since knowing her, I accepted her unconditionally . . . she was grandma!

On the other hand . . . the image of wrinkled skin and gray hair made grandmother-hood and old age unappealing, as did the word "menopause," which to me heralded the beginning of the end.

My friendship with Jessica lasted as we grew into adults, married our husbands, had babies, and moved on with our lives. My thirties turned into my forties and, all of a sudden, grandmother-hood! I was forty-two when I was presented with my first two grandchildren.

At the time, I was a divorced career woman and not dating. I was also fighting a losing battle with my weight, always adding and subtracting the same ten pounds, worked twelve to fourteen hours a day, and had nothing in my closet to wear except uniforms for work and jeans for my days off. My hair was dull and needed attention . . . "I'll get to it this weekend, for sure" being one of my mantras.

My life was twisting and turning, trying to find a good fit, so I was unprepared for this stage of my life. With ambivalence, I slid into midlife . . . the fear of wrinkles and gray hair swirling up from deep within.

I became more observant of the subtle gray strands interspersed with the rich brown of my hair. I leaned closer to the mirror each morning and every night, counting and recounting the lines that had not yet begun to form. I started used facial masks and mud packs, following the directions to a younger-looking me.

The first sign of menopause reared its head in the form of insomnia at the age of forty-five. I was used to getting a solid eight hours every night, and when that started to elude me . . .

I began to get cranky. I had less patience and energy and eventually wound up at the doctor's office to see why this was happening to me. He diagnosed premenopausal syndrome and sent me home with a prescription for sleeping pills. Never having taken anything to make me sleep, I was unprepared for the coma-like sleep that night and the drug-hazed state I was in the following morning.

"I can't take this crap! I need to function," I said to my reflection in the mirror and flushed the contents of the pill bottle down the toilet. I decided to go the diet route and stopped ingesting caffeine. I must have been crazy to give up my coffee and Snickers bars (my afternoon snack at work), but I did and it helped a lot. I never did get back to eight hours a night, but five undisturbed hours did just as well.

One evening, following a particularly busy shift at work, some friends and I decided to go out for dinner. After we filed into the restaurant, took a window booth, and gave our orders to the server, we got into a discussion about grandchildren. Growing up with only one image of how grandmas looked, I was unprepared for the way these grandmas looked. All but one of the women sitting with me were grandmothers. A few even had teenaged grandchildren, yet they didn't look any older than I did.

They started to impart some tips and advice on how to be a grandmother on our own terms and no one else's. As I became more observant, I noticed a few more things. The grandmothers of today didn't have gray hair unless they chose to, wearing it coiffed in a rich, soft silver.

"Yes, girl . . . Paul and I make love outside in the hot tub . . . it's a nice way to end the day . . . know what I mean?" one woman said and when she winked, we all erupted into peals of laughter, causing a few heads to turn.

They are also career women like me, some of them divorced and dating younger men, not to feel younger but because they can. Those who are married make their husbands feel twenty years younger . . . making uninhibited love, anytime, anywhere.

When you think about it, we have L'Oreal, Jenny Craig, and Revlon to thank for helping women the world over put a more vibrant look to this special time in our lives. Grandmas are living longer, going back to school, and contributing more than just yarn fluff to their families and communities.

We travel alone or, at times, take the grandchildren with us . . . especially when Disney World is our itinerary. We can give the children back to their parents, all sticky-fingered and ready for a bath . . . no guilt there as we slide into our own bath, warm and scented . . . candles glowing and sipping a glass of wine, in preparation for our evening . . . no matter what we had planned.

We play video games with our grandchildren and sex games with our lovers; wear pantyhose and pumps instead of rolled-down stockings and sensible shoes. We have personal ads online and in print, drive sports cars, inline skate, and scuba dive.

I will never be one of the many sitting in a nursing home, a body withered from years of neglect, its spirit caught in a shell, begging for release. My soul will never peer out through wrinkle-enshrouded eyes trying to capture the attention of someone—anyone willing to stop and listen.

Instead, I'll capture his attention across a crowded room. When going to work, I'll carry my attaché out to the car, my high heels clicking in my haste. I'll tuck my above-the-knee skirt beneath hosiery-encased thighs and position myself in the driver's seat, making my way to a job I have by choice and not by circumstance. When I get home, I'll slip into something comfortable and sip a cold beer straight from the bottle.

Now that I have arrived at the grandmother stage, I can honestly say that not all grandmas have gray hair—only those who want it. By keeping positive and true to myself, I have made this stage of my life into what I want it to be—fun, enlightening, and rewarding.

Two Women Walking

by Davi Walders

Our shadows and the bundle from the pound lead us. Walking as women have always walked, we are walking and talking, the way we have for twenty years, toward the next corner, down the next block, past porches, front doors, between pin oaks and maples. Words carry us beyond the street, beyond our feet, calves, and knees. They are our pulse. We listen for each other's vital signs, a voice tightening, a hesitation, a lost thread. Our eyes focus on the horizon. Words have etched us into each other; we balance without glancing. Like Picasso's lines, our voices are enough.

Walking is staying alive. Staying alive is walking. There were times we didn't walk. Times when things were twisted, broken—an ankle, a knee, the day my mother died, the night the dog succumbed, the week the marriage ended. Then we sat *shiva* (period of mourning), or over a beer, still and silent, without walking, without words, watching each other's eyes fill. But walking is also healing, so we continued. We have stepped over cracks, tree trunks, and dog droppings, waded through flooded streets and high grass, been delayed by pouting children, hurried by storm clouds and bared dog teeth, sideswiped by joggers and

bikers. But mostly we have kept our own pace, the pace of wan-
derers, and our own place, the middle of deserted streets.
Claiming space and time for our words and our weight, our
hopes and our hearts, for staying alive.

Walking is magic. We have learned to read the signs. When
childhood is often a matter of survival, magic must wait. Now
we walk in magic time, following a hairy woodpecker's mating
call, searching branches, telephone wires, our necks arched
until they ache. Watching clouds, catching a zoo of dancing
white tigers, crocodiles, even a floating badger. Finding a dime
at dusk, but only one, until a few steps later, finding another.
Eight pennies once. That was easier; they could be divided.
Gloves, red, pink, white, memories of mothers, confusions,
encouragements. Paper clips, two, three, green, red, jumbos and
butterflies, waiting, leading us, daring us to unlock files, sort
closets, leave careers, remember, re-create our histories. We
watch for signs as we walk, pocketing found objects, finding
ourselves.

Walking is not always easy, even when we keep our eyes on
the path. We have slipped on ice patches, stepped in puddles
deeper than our boots, caught a foot in a pothole, hanging on
to each other until both limb and shoe were liberated.
Sometimes we bump into each other, losing sight of the separate shadows leading us. We have frozen and thawed, thrown
back our heads and howled at the sky, sat on a bench and just
cried, making our way, reworking our words along many paths.
Knowing the neighborhood trails well, we need no destination.
Walking is always heading home . . . one tail wagging, two
shadows following, four shoes ambling, two voices connecting,
one conversation . . . for twenty years. ❧

A Celebration of Wrinkles

by Jan Andersen

A short while ago, my partner and I were watching a rather graphic documentary about cosmetic surgery, which covered the individual profiles of four people who had chosen to put their faces and bodies at the disposal of a plastic surgeon and his knives. As we watched the slicing, the sucking, the tugging, and the stapling, my partner said, "Why would anyone want to go to such drastic lengths to have all the character removed from their face?"

I think it is important to mention here that my partner is just thirty years old and I am forty-two. I have twelve years' more wear and tear in my face and in the lines around my eyes to indicate that I have endured the stresses and strains of life by laughing in the face of adversity. My partner lovingly tells me that every line, freckle, and feature—whether or not I consider it to be a flaw—contributes toward making me who I am, where I've been, and what I've done. To erase those characteristics would be like editing my life and removing the memories and experiences, both good and bad, that have been etched on my face.

Who was it that first decided that young and smooth was more beautiful than mature and furrowed? The wisdom of maturity can be just as attractive as the innocence of youth, and the number of wrinkles that you have doesn't always reveal your age. It's all a matter of attitude. I recently met a woman who had had a facelift, together with a few nips and tucks here and there. Whilst I don't deny that she was attractive, her face was expressionless and reminded me of that of an inanimate shop mannequin's glossy, untarnished surface, with a total absence of personality. Despite the lack of creases and slack skin, however, she didn't look younger than her years. In fact, I was surprised when she revealed her age, because I was under the impression that she was older. *My* grandmother, on the other hand, was one of those fair-skinned types, like me, whose skin was not as resilient as some—and yet, although her face was deeply lined, she still looked twenty years younger. She was vibrant and energetic, with a child-like outlook, a wicked sense of humor, and the gait of someone in her thirties.

Were it not for the media insensitively setting the definition of beauty and the framework for acceptability, a lot more people would be happy to grow old gracefully and welcome each new wrinkle with dignity and delight.

Many years ago, I remember watching a particularly unsettling episode of *The Twilight Zone,* entitled "The Eye of the Beholder," in which a beautiful girl (at least what we perceive as beautiful) lived in a world inhabited by people with pig-like faces. They were regarded as normal, whereas she was branded as "ugly" and a "freak," which caused her to embark on a series of surgical operations to change her face so that she would fit into their society. When the operations failed, she was banished to an outcast village to live with others of her kind.

The above story may seem extreme, but many women and men resort to radical measures to enhance their appearance, seek approval, and consequently feel more valued by modern-day society. If wrinkles and maturity were suddenly in vogue, would plastic surgeons be inundated with demands for lines to be carved into faces and necks and eager requests for jawline implants to give the dropping jowl effect? Would everyone roast themselves in the sun without caution and wash their faces in detergent to help promote aged, leathery skin?

Of course, the reason that ageism continues is, firstly, because the ageist members of our society are those who don't belong to the age group against which they are discriminating and, secondly, because the media hasn't yet cottoned on to the fact that maturity and wrinkles can equate to beauty and desirability. After all, the most beautiful homes and the most beautiful scenery inevitably have character. Compare the blank canvas of a fresh, magnolia-painted house to a period cottage, with nooks, crannies, and higgledy-piggledy beams, and you tell me which one has more character. Look at the pure but empty expanses of the Antarctic and then view a craggy mountain range on the continent, and think about which scene you would like to view on a long-term basis.

Isn't it about time that people were viewed in the same way? Instead of dreading the aging process, we could all look forward to growing more beautiful with each passing year and to greeting each new line, blemish, or mole as a beauty-enhancing feature, rather than an unattractive sign of moving from youth through to antiquity. 🦋

Was That Menopause?

by Gail Kavanagh

as that menopause? There must have been a lot going on in my life while it was happening because I barely noticed it.

But it's only now—now that I know it is over—that I have learned to stop dreading it.

I remember thinking, at about forty-five, that it would be all downhill from here. My children would grow up, I would shrivel up, and all the energy and power I had enjoyed for so many years would just wither away.

Yes, that was very dramatic of me—but dramatizing isn't just confined to teenagers, you know. And I had heard so many horror stories about menopause from older women who had treated the whole process like a terminal illness. Terminal, that is, to their womanhood, their youth, their hopes, and their dreams. When I was twenty-one, an older person who fancied himself a wise mentor told me, "From now on, all the days will seem like short summers."

No, they didn't. Some days seemed like long dark winters, others were brilliant, far better than I had ever known. But they didn't pass any quicker or slower because I had come of age. But the menopause wisdom seemed very plausible. I had no older sisters or aunts to pass on their experiences, and my mother had had a hysterectomy in her thirties, so her experience of the end of childbearing had been colored by that.

It wasn't actually the end of my childbearing years that I feared. Marriage to a small, dark, and handsome man had blessed me with seven children, and so I felt I had celebrated my fertility enough. But I defined myself as a healthy, vigorous woman in the prime of life—fit and able to run around after all those kids. In my forties, I still had children at school and a busy home life. My older children were experiencing the teenage years and young adulthood with all the usual drama, and I was packing school lunches, warming up the car, solving last-minute hair and boyfriend crises, all before 9 A.M.

Somewhere in all this, the event that I had been dreading started. At first, of course, I thought I was pregnant. When that didn't prove to be the case, I thought I must have been dieting too much.

On and off, I was reminded that I might be, as they used to say, at a Certain Time of Life, but then everything returned to normal again and I went on sorting out the washing.

When my youngest child turned nine, I returned to journalism, working at a local newspaper. Looking back, I am sure that I must have been going through menopause then too, but I was simply too busy to notice.

And I continued to dread it. The feminist writer Germaine Greer had published a book on menopause, which I refused to read because the reviews suggested it upheld all my worst fears.

"How am I going to cope with that on top of all this?" I would wonder, as I rushed home from work to my mother's place to pick up my youngest children, and then home to start dinner. Life was just so busy, and thankfully I was still hale and hearty enough to deal with it all. Menopause would rob me of that, I was sure; it was the gateway to old age.

I can't even remember when I became aware that my monthly cycle had stopped completely. Perhaps around the time my older daughters were getting married, or when they were expecting their first babies. Looking back, I can see that there was a long period of time between when I first began to suspect menopause was on the horizon, and when I knew for sure that it had actually happened.

I got hot flashes, of course, although it took a while for me to realize that it was a hot flash and not just the results of rushing around in our hot Australian weather. I did a fair bit of crying, I suppose—both happy tears (my daughters got married and gave birth to my beautiful grandchildren) and sad tears.

It is only now that I realize with finality that I had actually gone through menopause and that I have since started my third lifetime as a woman. First the child, then the young woman, and now the crone. Except that I don't have time to feel like an old, wise crone dishing out advice to all and sundry, whether they ask for it or not. I have all these grandchildren—eight at the last headcount and two on the way. I have cut back on my day job, it is true, but only so I can segue into full-time freelance writing. I have spent ten years in the workforce, and now I want to be home again.

Writing this is actually the first time I have thought about menopause in ages. It has come, and gone, and I am still busy, vigorous, and trying to get organized. None of what I feared has come to pass, and I can finally put that irrational dread behind me. I took no medication, no HRT, no medical intervention of any kind. I have always eaten a healthy diet, needing to keep up my strength for all those kids, but as I have grown older, I tend to eat more salads and vegetables. I have taken a multivitamin supplement for years, and I walk regularly, now that I don't have young children to chase around (except when my grandchildren are here).

I don't know if any of this was a factor, or if I simply was too busy to notice it, or worry about the symptoms.

And I discovered, talking to other women, that my experience was not that unique. A work colleague who has also gone through menopause has never looked or felt better. Kerry brushed off the hot flashes with her usual sense of humor—"Is it hot today, or is it just me?"—and is entering this new stage of her life with energy and purpose. She is following her long-held dream of living in the country on a small holding.

Another friend, who did need medical help and loving support for the symptoms of menopause, still has discovered new energy and interests with the end of her childbearing years. Now she and her daughter plan to open a shop, something she has dreamed of for years. What we all had in common was a dread of the event, brought on by "popular wisdom" and horror stories heard in our youth. But when it actually happened, it turned out to be just another stage of life, like adolescence, with its own challenges and rewards.

I feel like Peggy Lee, who recorded a great song called "Is That All There Is?"

Is that all there is to menopause? Well, it is for me. 🕭

The Changes That Come with "The Change"

by Martha Conte

Better late than never. Better to grow up at the age of fifty than never grow up at all. Perpetual adolescence is not usually associated with women, but there are those of us "stuck in time" out there in the female population.

For many years, I was unaware of my "inner teenager."

My personality was serious and shy. My actions, I felt, did not meet the criteria of immature behavior. I did not attend a constant round of parties; was not always in dire financial straits because of impulsive spending; and did not have a new romantic partner every week. My employers considered me a good, reliable employee—until I grew bored with the job and quit.

I changed jobs about every three years. As this pattern continued, I saw it not as a problem, but as an adventure. Like many members of my baby-boomer generation, I was trying to "find myself" and find the "meaning of life."

"When are you going to settle down?" my aunt asked, when I informed her I had changed jobs again. "Maybe now," I replied. But I did not settle down. I still had not found the right job, the right career, and the right person to marry. My standard joke to others was, "I have trouble making commitments" and deliberately stuttering while saying what I called the "c" word.

The years passed. I zipped through all the milestone birthdays with ease—thirty, no problem; forty, no midlife crisis. My forty-fifth birthday did not faze me. Finally a birthday came that caught my attention.

I turned fifty years old. Physically, I felt fine. Emotionally, I was stunned.

"Half a century! Middle aged!" I said out loud to myself in the mirror that morning. "In ten more years, I'll be sixty!" Where did the time go?

Mourning the loss of my youth as one would the death of a loved one, I went through the five stages of grief: denial—this can't be happening to me; anger—how dare the American Association of Retired Persons send me an invitation to join their organization; bargaining—I'll change my ways if I can have my youth back; depression—my life is over; acceptance—I stopped coloring my hair.

As my gray hairs emerged, so did the reality of my life. I had not achieved what I wanted, career and financial success. Now what? Some changes had to be made, and this effort required the "c" word.

Commitment is no longer a dirty word. I have committed myself to my place of employment, no matter how bored I may get. I have learned to find joy and challenge in the simplest of tasks, both in the workplace and at home.

I have committed myself to a healthier lifestyle. Growing older is easier when your body is in good shape.

I have committed myself to being responsible with my finances. I do not want to be an eighty-year-old bag lady.

I have committed myself to my spirituality. It is comforting to acknowledge a Higher Power greater than oneself. Now the meaning of life matters less than living it to the fullest.

I have always wanted to start my part-time business, and now I am committed to this goal. What helps me in making this life transition are the fruits of middle age. I now know myself very well. I know my strengths, weaknesses, and talents. I possess a confidence and surety I never had when I was in my twenties.

And this is a good time to be in midlife. Our generation is fortunate to have information about middle age and menopause—topics taboo for discussion in my mother's generation—publicly available. Pharmaceutical and consumer products exist to assist us with the many challenges we face now.

As for my experience with menopause, I found it easier than turning fifty. I am one of those people whose internal body thermostat is set high, and I live in a part of the country with a year-round warm climate. I was never able to distinguish among a hot flash, hot weather, or just me overheating. The end of my menstrual cycle was cause for celebration. Back in high school, we gals referred to that time of the month as "your friend" or "the curse." I had a lifetime of difficult periods, and my menstrual cycle was no friend. I am delighted to finally be free from this curse. No more planning of events around my menstrual cycle or disruption of events because of it. That makes me feel young again. ❧

Friendship's Return

by Amy Lynch

t's a cold morning, rainy and dark. I cross the deck of the coffeehouse, shake out my umbrella and go inside. My friend, Beth, is reading the newspaper at our usual corner table. She looks up and smiles. And all at once, I'm warm.

If you're connecting more deeply with your friends lately, you're not alone. Somewhere around age forty to forty-five, most of us begin craving more friendships with other women. Psychologist Terri Apter, author of *Secret Paths: Women in the New Midlife,* found that during this stage of our lives we talk about our female friendships nearly as much as adolescent girls do. Women in their thirties talk about friends only half this often.

Why, as we enter the second half of our lives, do we become as giddy as schoolgirls about female friends? The answer is "identity"—just as it was when we were teens. Midlife is a period of transformation. As we re-create ourselves and find new direction for our lives, decisions must be made and dreams brought to light. And we turn, again, to female friends. Much as we love our partners, children, siblings, and parents, they often have a vested interest in seeing us stable and unchanging. A good friend is more likely to understand our yearning to grow and our resistance to the roles and limits we've accepted in the past. With her we're free to ask, "How do you see me?" and "Who do you think I might become?" At some point during midlife, perhaps at several points, we gather ourselves for a great leap forward. Our very futures depend on amassing enough energy and support to sustain the leap. That's why I don't just enjoy meeting my friend Beth for breakfast—some part of me needs to.

Time is scarce in her life and in mine, yet we meet regularly to sit across the table from each other, listening and telling our stories. She is a walking record of my life these days, knows about my yo-yo marriage, my stop-and-start career. Not that Beth has experienced these things herself. Single and successful, she built a business while I was changing diapers.

· · ·

Our moms could reasonably expect to share a predictable timeline—school, marriage, children, an empty nest, and retirement years—with their women friends. Not you and me. Age and stage no longer match. Some women my age (forty-eight) have kids in graduate school. Others are flying to China to adopt little girls. In her research, Sandy Sheehy, the author of *Connecting: The Enduring Power of Female Friendship,* found that understanding each other's life events, rather than sharing them, cements midlife friendships. During our forties and fifties we become increasingly likely to develop friends who are not like us—women who are older or younger, or who took a different path. At this stage, says Sheehy, a woman's friends reflect the sides of herself a woman wants to explore, express, or recapture and the kind of support she needs to heal old wounds or meet present challenges. These are decades when we seek out friends who help us stretch into new selves, reflecting our possibilities more than they do our pasts.

I used to be in awe of Beth. She was so skinny and successful. So free. Flying off to conferences and workshops, flying to another city for an evening's date. Little did I know how she longed for a committed relationship, or that she often wondered if she should have a child.

• • •

Researchers find that during early adulthood, most women put their energy into romantic attachment, careers, or children. Friends are around as touchstones, but they usually aren't central to our lives. Apter suggests that this is because young women are just learning how difficult and messy life really is. They're still striving for perfection—to be perfect businesswomen, perfect wives or mothers—and they withdraw from other women in order to hide their failings.

Thank goodness we get over it. None of us has perfect lives, and as we mature we care less and less if others know it. In their research, both Apter and Sheehy found women with a few decades behind them using the word "relief" repeatedly when they described their friendships. Somewhere along the way we let go of envy and pretense. We begin judging other women more leniently, and we relax, knowing they judge us more kindly, too.

Our hour is slipping away. There's lipstick on our coffee mugs. Beth tells a story about losing her temper, something she does often. And me, I'm melodramatic to a fault. But that's shrugged off at our little table, forgiveness a given. We're occupied with other tasks, with cheering each other on and holding each other up. I glance at my watch. Time to go. We always hug now, when we part. ✿

The Merry Recluse

by Caroline Knapp

Not long ago, in the locker room of my gym, I eavesdropped on a woman as she spoke about her upcoming wedding. We're thinking about a honeymoon in Hawaii, she said. We're registering at Bloomingdale's. We're buying a new car. We're doing A, B, and C. We, we, *we.* I stood there, thinking about how infrequently I use plural pronouns to describe the events of my life, and I felt a familiar stab of inadequacy, questions about priorities and social worth scratching at the subconscious. On the broad spectrum of solitude, I lean toward the extreme end. I work alone, as well as live alone, so I can pass an entire day without uttering so much as a hello to another human being. Sometimes a day's conversation consists of only five words, uttered at the local Starbucks: "Large coffee with milk, please." I also work out alone, I grocery shop alone, and I cook and eat and watch television alone. If you don't count the dog (I do; many don't), I sleep alone at night and wake up alone every morning. Much of the time I don't question this state of affairs—it just is. But I listened to this woman in the gym, I spun out a vivid fantasy about her life (the best friend at the next StairMaster, the colleagues at the office, the fiancé at home, the 200 friends and family members at the wedding reception, the children two or three years hence), and I felt like an alien, a member of some mutant species getting dressed in the locker room before crawling back to her dark, solitary cave.

Why don't I want that? That's what comes up. Why do I find the fantasy—husband, family, kids—exhausting instead of alluring? *Is* there something wrong with me? Do I have a life?

In fact, that woman at the gym, poised as she is at the matrimonial brink, is not necessarily headed for a more "normal" life than the one I lead. For the first time, there are as many single-person households in the United States as there are married couples with children—25 percent of the population in each camp—but in moments like that I understand that cultural standards and expectations haven't quite caught up with the numbers. Census figures be damned: If you choose to be alone, you're destined to spend a certain amount of time wondering why.

I suppose the why, at least for me, is internal, temperamental, as deeply personal as sexuality. Like most women, I grew up expecting to marry someday, expecting to have a family, expecting to want babies. And, like some women (and men), I've found that the years have passed and passed and passed and those things simply haven't happened, as though some deeper yearning simply failed to kick in. Lots of life decisions are made that way. Choices are revealed by default, answers arrived at far more passively than we might expect. I look up today and realize, with some surprise, that I've spent the bulk of my adult life alone—fifteen of the last eighteen years. For much of that time—indeed, until my merry little epiphany in the kitchen—I've tended to see my solitary status as a transient state, a product of circumstance instead of a matter of style. In fact, I suspect I've lived this way for a reason, that the degree of solitude I've chosen feeds me in some way, that the fit—me with me—is right.

Considered in that light, the "why"—why spend so much time alone?—becomes a more interesting question: why *not?* I've always been drawn to solitude, felt a kind of luxurious relief in its self-generated pace and rhythms. I eat breakfast pretty much 'round the clock—muffins in the morning, scones for lunch, cereal at night—which may be odd but is also oddly satisfying, if only because the choice is my own. I am master of my own clutter, king of the television remote, author of every detail, large and quirky. The passenger seat of my car, uninhabited by humans most of the time, will always be a disaster area, a repository of cassette tapes and empty coffee cups and errant dog toys; my alarm clock will always blast National Public Radio at precisely 6:02; my ashtrays (smoking permitted here constantly) will always be blessedly full and stinky. Solitude is a breeding ground for idiosyncrasy, and I relish that about it, the way it liberates within.

Of course, living alone can make you psycho, too. I often feel deranged in the supermarket, hunting down grazeable foodstuffs that don't come in family-size packages, wishing I could buy grapes in bags of ten so that the other eighty don't rot in the refrigerator, wondering if the check-out clerk has noticed my apparent obsession with wheat flakes. The lack of backup can overwhelm the solitary dweller, especially when you're confronted with life's more fearsome tasks (decoding assembly instructions, killing spiders); the lack of distraction, which alters your core relationship to physical space, can make you think you're nuts.

The other night, I caught myself talking to a spoon, which had twice fallen off the counter and clattered onto the tile. "Hey!" I said. "Stop doing that!" And then I stood there and shook my head, aware of that tiny persistent question, the low-level mosquito whine inside: *Is this normal¿ Is it¿*

For me, the most pressing challenge involves negotiating the line between solitude and isolation, which can be very thin indeed. Social skills are like muscles, subject to atrophy, and I find I have to be as careful about maintaining human contact as I am about maintaining physical health. Drop below a certain level of contact with other humans, and the simplest social activities—meeting someone for coffee, going out to dinner—begin to seem monumental and scary and exhausting, the interpersonal equivalent of trying to swim to France. Solitude is often most comforting, most sustaining, when it's enjoyed in relation to other humans; fail to strike the right balance and life gets a little surreal. You start dreaming about television characters as though they were real people; houseflies start to feel companionable; minor occasions that others find perfectly ordinary (the arrival of a houseguest, an evening requiring anything dressier than sweatpants) start to feel bizarre and unfathomable.

And yet I'd be hard pressed to leave this little world, singular and self-constructed as it is. I have lived in the Land of We; at times, I have pounded on the door for admission, frantic with worry and need. When the friend at dinner asked me how it felt not to be in a relationship, I remembered all too clearly what it was like to feel despair at the state, to regard my own company as scary and inferior. When I see that look of discomfort come over my friend Wendy as I talk about my unplanned weekends, I remember how horrifying I once found the concept of unstructured time, how much difficulty I've had simply sitting still, giving my own emotions room to surface. And when I hear people pepper their speech with the word "we" like that woman in the gym, I remember a lot of painful years spent struggling to define myself in relation to other people, as though my own existence didn't count unless it was attached to someone else's.

That night in my kitchen, fixing my Kellogg's feast, reveling in the order and quiet of my own home, felt like a gift, a victory of sorts, an awareness that some of those struggles have receded further into the past. I am shy by nature, a person who's always found something burdensome about human interaction and who probably always will, at least to some degree. Accordingly, I have always felt a deep relief in solitude, but I've not always been able to *bask* in it, to sit alone in a room without getting edgy, to feel that comfort and solace and validation are available outside the paradigm of a romance, to believe that my own resources—my own company, my own choices—can power me through the dark corridors of solitude and into the brightness.

I took my cereal bowl into the living room, settled down in front of the television, and thought, so merrily: *I'm home.* ❧

Some Age-Old Advice:
Carpe the Midlife Crisis

by Mary Schmich

*L*et us now praise the midlife crisis.

A midlife crisis is a perfectly reasonable, even useful, response to the urgent thought that flashes in many a midlife brain: I Am Going to Die. Anyone who reaches the middle of life and doesn't at least briefly shriek and shudder at this thought isn't paying attention.

A midlife crisis feels lousy at the time, so you don't necessarily realize while you're in it that it's the water break in the middle of the long journey. It's the pause that could refresh your life or even save it. It's the startling moment you realize you need to switch maps.

But if you read about a MacArthur Foundation study released this week, you'd think the time-honored midlife crisis doesn't even exist. You'd think it was a myth of advertisers and self-help authors. From the media hype, you'd think that only six freaks had ever suffered this mortifying affliction.

How absurd. I am here to report that the midlife crisis is alive and well and we're all better off for it.

Nothing is more annoying—or less believable—than the midlife person who says, "I never think about my age." What a pity. Life is short. Age is real. Think about it.

Parents die. Children grow up. The body fails. Your job is what it is, or it isn't. There's a vast world out there you haven't seen. More than 1.2 million good books you haven't read and never will.

Every midlife person I know is having or has had a midlife crisis in response to such thoughts. That doesn't mean they're miserable. It just means they're awake. And sometimes they're awake in the middle of the night, sensibly asking themselves: What am I doing? What have I done? How can I best use the time I have left? If not now, when? And should I color my hair?

Questions are at the heart of a midlife crisis, and questions are rarely comfortable. But you have to ask the questions to find the answers. Many of us have to pass through crisis to arrive at calm.

I know people whose midlife crises have taken them on odd trips. Seeking to answer the big questions, they've run marathons, taken up yoga, started going to church, put more soy in their diet, changed jobs, had chaotic love affairs. These were people in crisis, though they might not have called it that.

If declaring the midlife crisis a myth eases the stigma of middle age, okay. Middle age needs some good PR. For too long, "middle-age" has been an insult.

But the midlife crisis is part of the process of learning that midlife has many charms. One of those charms is the ability to hold two contradictory views of life at once. You can say in one breath: "I hate being in my forties (or fifties or sixties)," and swear in the next, "I'd never go back to my thirties (or twenties or teens)."

You can miss your youthful body but be grateful you'll never have to return to your youthful anxieties. You can sigh over your shrinking possibilities and be glad you're no longer confused by so much choice. You can feel a twinge of regret for roads not taken even as you happily head down seductive new roads you'd never noticed before.

Last summer I was at the beach with an old college friend. "Let's go swimming!" he said. It was a windy day. The water was freezing. I cringed.

"You're getting old," he taunted. "I remember when you would have jumped into that ocean stark naked in the middle of winter." This was an exaggeration, but better to have your youth exaggerated than forgotten.

"You're right," I said. "I am getting old. And in redefining my pleasures, I'm not going to do something I don't want to do just to prove I'm still twenty-two."

Of course, I did go in the ocean, just to prove I wasn't old. But in that moment, I had one of those midlife self-help epiphanies. The middle of life shouldn't be about repeating past pleasures just to prove you're young. It should be about discovering what really pleases you at this age.

Many people have to go through a crisis to figure out the pleasures of the second half. So? So have the courage of your midlife crisis. Be wise enough to feel that foolish. And remember that however old you are today, tomorrow it will seem young. 🔊

The I of the Beholder

by Sarah Shapiro

The feminist Germaine Greer once described an unpleasant lunch hour she'd had in a trendy Manhattan restaurant. For three decades a figure of some renown and influence in the American women's movement, Ms. Greer was finding it difficult to get her waiter's attention that afternoon.

As she sat there impatiently trying to catch his eye—*any* waiter's eye—she noticed that at various tables around the room, a number of other women, younger than she, weren't having the same problem. In fact, at the next table over, not only was a waiter responding diligently to a good-looking diner's every request, but to make matters worse, the young woman in question was accompanied for lunch by an enthralled middle-aged man, someone just about Germaine Greer's own age.

That's when it hit her, said Greer: *She'd become invisible.*

Surely that's not the only time a waiter's unresponsiveness has triggered an existential crisis of the highest order, a woman's encounter with her own nothingness that not even transcendental meditation can provide. For the female who has absorbed—from childhood and adolescence on—the notion that to get a man's attention is to have evidence that she exists, watching her beauty ebb and fade is to preside helplessly over the disappearance of her very own self. To be invisible to the male gaze is to not be there at all.

If the universal human need to *be there*—in other words, to be recognized, noticed, taken seriously—is intertwined primarily in a woman's mind and heart with her power to attract, she'll be getting some uncomfortable wake-up calls somewhere along the line. As we all know, and try heroically to deny, we have every reason to trust that our bodies will get weaker and uglier as time goes by. We can successfully forestall the onset of this preprogrammed deterioration with exercise and cosmetic surgery and nutrition and makeup, but eventually the bathroom mirror will start sending daily bulletins about our unbelievable transformation into our grandparents.

As the saying goes, inside every old person is a young one wondering what the hell happened; throughout history, women have sought to be beautiful and have appraised their value accordingly. Yet in our times, there's something particularly obsessive and twisted about how these natural inclinations manifest themselves. The increasingly widespread occurrence among middle-aged women of eating disorders— pity my generation—gives eloquent expression to the war against one's own self that can occur when the powerful twin longings, for love and for transcendence, are channeled primarily into the quest to preserve one's youth and beauty. If that pursuit takes place in the absence of any other equally authentic and viable philosophy of self, our body's condition and appearance become the most tangible measure of our worth.

For better and for worse, I'm no exception. My own childhood was populated by female authority figures who seemed to have something other than their figures in mind, but I myself just will not go gently into that good night. As a baby-boomer, I insist, absolutely insist, that time does not go by, and I'd rather die than appear in the clothes my grandmother wore at my age.

How can we get free of the petty tyrannies of our female vanity? Short of reincarnation as a man, one way out would be a nun-like withdrawal from the world, whereby we'd be free to cultivate our inner lives without outside interference. Another would be to adopt the Saudi Arabian style of obliteration of one's female form and individuality altogether.

Another would be to live in such a way that our self-presentation conveys this idea to ourselves and others: My identity is not equal to my reflection in a three-way bathroom mirror.

• • •

Years ago, when in-flight movies were still being projected onto a single screen at the head of the cabin, I had just demurely declined to partake of El Al's audio system when *Thelma and Louise* came on. I was soon scurrying down the aisle in search of that stewardess bearing earphones upon a tray. Even without sound, the plot already had me hooked.

The story went like this. Two pretty working-class women, one in her thirties, the other in her forties, try desperately to escape the stultifying confines of their limited existence. Their respective lowlife mates see them not as people with deeply felt hopes and dreams, but—surprise!—as sex objects.

Along with the final cut—in which Thelma and Louise sail off a cliff in their car rather than suffer any more of the world's cruel misunderstandings and humiliations—one other scene from that affecting film remains in my mind's eye today.

Under a baking sun somewhere out West, the two of them are speeding down a desert highway in an open convertible. Exhilarated to the point of ecstasy at having successfully fled boyfriend, husband, and murderously monotonous jobs, they're singing their heads off, throwing back their heads in laughter, and with weather permitting, shedding as much of their clothing as the PG rating allows.

Suddenly comes a crude intrusion upon their newborn joy. A huge Mack truck is bearing down upon them, pulling up alongside so that its leering driver can honk and wink obscenely and utter raw come-ons from his higher perch. The women's bliss is sullied, their newfound liberty gravely injured. Enraged at being painfully diminished in this all-too-familiar manner, and by everything in their past that is evoked for them by his obtuse greeting, they set in screaming, "Would you say that to your sister?" and then proceed to indulge in a retaliatory assault until the frightened brute, much to his dumb astonishment, gets a real run for his money.

We in our economy-class seats delighted in his comeuppance, but after landing at Ben-Gurion Airport, a few obvious questions did linger in my own mind. Were street-smart Thelma and Louise too naive in the ways of the world to realize that dressing like that would attract such a man's attention? Were they feigning ignorance? Not to come to a boor's defense, but wasn't he responding predictably under the circumstances? Was it only the truck driver's superficial view of them that had defined them as objects, or was it also their own self-presentation?

The two women, in flight from their culture and heading precariously toward the unknown, could have taken an inward turn into the infinite expanse of their unexplored spiritual selves. But with no road, that they could see, to lead them in that direction, they chose death instead of growth.

What's lost when one can pass unnoticed? The truest joys are those that, by nature, require privacy to blossom, and the most enduring accomplishments those that go unseen by others.

To the extent that we see ourselves more as bodies than as souls, to that extent are we vulnerable to what is quaintly called "the ravages of time." To the extent that we seek beauty in our reflections rather than our deeds, to that extent are we blind to the myriad beauties that surround us.

And to the extent that we struggle to hold the world's gaze, to that extent will our bathroom mirrors increasingly chastise us, day by day, for neglecting our inner lives, invisible but to ourselves and God. ❧

The Allure of Invisibility

by Miriam Weiss

Sophie reveled in it. Georgina felt complimented. Allison would laugh or giggle girlishly. Most of my friends loved the whistles, the hooting, the crude invitations that came from male spectators as they strutted the sidewalks in their teens and their twenties. I, however, never wanted any part of it. This kind of male attention made me feel weird. It made me feel violated. It made me feel raped.

Perhaps the fact that I had lived in a sequestered and religious community prior to my foray into the "outside world" and had attended an all-girls parochial school explained a large part of my discomfort. I did not know how to relate to boys, and I didn't understand the dynamics of male-female interaction. I was a total innocent. In retrospect, I probably thought that the male species was just a different variation of the female. I was naive about the all-powerful stream of sexuality that surged and swirled and insinuated itself into every aspect of male-female relations, into the tiniest minutiae of everyday life. Or perhaps the source of my discomfort lay in the sudden and unexpected attention I was now garnering, after a lifetime of being ignored. All my life I had been overweight and homely.

At nineteen, I lost thirty pounds, put on contact lenses, straightened both my hair and my nose, and suddenly turned into a butterfly. I was unprepared for the dramatically different way that men now reacted to me, and it didn't make me happy; it made me mad.

The doorman at the office building where I worked in Manhattan had never acknowledged me before my physical transformation. Reared to be polite, I had always greeted him with a cheery "Good morning," but he had looked away in disinterest. My metamorphosis, however, not only changed me, it changed *him.* His manner toward me did a 360-degree turn as he became downright unctuous: radiating sunny smiles, oozing charm, solicitous with little packages, overzealous in plying me with weather updates and other unnecessary information; joking, compliments, bending, bowing, scraping . . . it made me sick.

The exact same scenario happened at the local coffee shop with the counterman who had served me indifferently in the past but now stood attentive at my entrance; the deli owner whose behavior had previously been brusque and disgruntled but was now warm and effusive; even the local mailman, from whom I had never even merited a shrug in response to my daily hellos, now turned servile and ingratiating. Some people might argue that with the change in my physical appearance had come a concomitant change in my self-image and I myself was emitting different vibes. I considered this interpretation as I puzzled over my newfound attraction but ultimately rejected it as untrue. Women acted no differently toward me now, and *I* certainly did not act any differently toward men. No, it was my upgraded appearance—not my enhanced self-esteem—that was generating all this heat.

Perhaps other women would have simply luxuriated in all this male interest, at least those who, like me, had never experienced it before, but what I felt more than anything else was indignation. *I'm the same person I was before,* I obsessed, *the same essence, the same me, I just look a little different on the outside. What is this saying about men and the way they react to women⸮* I fumed. *Can't they respect me for who I am—inside⸮ My soul doesn't count⸮ My intellect means nothing⸮ My personality and heart and character and aspirations and ideals and values might as well fall by the wayside, just as long as I have a pretty face⸮*

"You know what you have to do to get the job⸮" a man winked at me once during an interview at a television station, sending me home in tears. "I just want to be seen as a *person,*" I wailed to my friends who—psychology majors all of them—thought I was squelching my sexuality, repressing my drives, sublimating my desires, and being dishonest with myself. "You are such a hypocrite!" they would explode when I would try to thrash out loud with them my discomposure at being so *seen,* so *visible* to men. They could not believe that I genuinely disliked the attention, that I felt embarrassed and anxious about being in the limelight.

I did *not* respond to this sudden awakening of interest in men. I did *not* respect those who were attentive now but had ignored me before. For these, I only felt contempt. Even my husband—one of the few men with whom I felt safe enough to be sexual—never understood why I studiously avoided construction sites and hard-hatters and crossed the street to flee the stomps, the shouts, the whistles, and the leers. He felt a certain pride that his wife elicited all this attention; I felt as if I were going to *die.*

Over the years, as I became more acclimated to living in a mixed-sex world, I learned invaluable lessons about relating to men. I learned *not* to engage in prolonged conversations with them when I met them at meetings or in social situations. I restrained myself from greeting them with the warmth I reserved for my female friends; I never offered to help with small favors or little kindnesses. I censured my speech and guarded my actions. Because, invariably, almost every single time I had done one of the above, it was misconstrued.

I hated restricting a significant part of myself. By nature, I am a warm, fuzzy, generous person, and it was a veritable feat to keep this part of me in check. But I felt that if I didn't, complications were likely to arise. As time wore on, I no longer felt *indignant*; I felt resentful, instead. It would have been nice to associate more with men, have them as friends, but I recognized that as long as I was young, attractive, and visible, sexuality stood stubbornly in the way.

About ten years ago, when I turned forty-two, I realized with a start that my allure was waning. When I walked by a group of men, they would no longer gyrate their bodies into pretzels and crane their necks after me; they didn't suddenly fall silent to gawk and leer as I approached; they no longer leaned out of car windows to undress me with their eyes as I sped by. Overnight, it seemed, I had suddenly and inexorably become that which I had always longed for: invisible.

My friends—aging along with me—lament their invisibility, step up their visits to the hairdresser, gym, and spa; talk about the merits of laser versus plastic. But I have to tell you, what *I* feel is *relief.* And, having graduated from being psychology majors twenty years ago to full-fledged psychologists today, my friends continue to take particular delight in analyzing me and my incongruous reaction to my untimely retirement as a sex object. Not for a minute do they accept my cavalier attitude; they are convinced I am playing possum or ostrich, in the throes of denial, defensiveness, disassociation of affect, or a combination of all three. As much as I try, I cannot convince them that I am sincere.

It's not that my thickening waistline, slackening skin, and labyrinth of lines underneath my eyes don't bother me. Of course they do, and I am no Pollyanna. But as my appearance matures and men's interest consequently flags, I find that I suddenly possess a certain freedom today that I never knew before, a freedom that I welcome and enjoy.

For the first time in my life, I am finally able to enter into the order of *men* as a full participant where I am viewed not as a babe, not as a potential girlfriend, not as a sex object to "come on to" or "hit upon" but as a human being, period. The barriers that sexuality erected in the past have fallen away, and since it is no longer a consideration, since *I* am no longer a consideration, I am now being seen as a full-fledged person. That means my opinions count, my ideas count, and *I* count in a way I never did before. At last, I can engage in the world and truly harness my power. As a "crone," I feel stronger, more influential and more capable of effecting true change, because I have finally been accepted into the club, am now a team player. Before, I was looked at a lot, but never genuinely *seen.* Having shed my identity as a sex object, I am now regarded in a whole different way.

Aside from being taken more seriously, there are other advantages that this new phase brings—rewards that I reap with relish. For the first time in my life, I can genuinely converse with men freely and uninhibitedly. I do not have to fear that any innocent remarks that I make will be misconstrued as sexual innuendo. I can now proffer little compliments to men—on their wisdom, their accomplishments, even on their appearances—as I do often and generously with my own female friends. I do not have to avoid certain subjects that might stray into forbidden-talk territory. Not only has my conversation loosened up, but my actions are freer, too. Today, I can freely dispense for men the little civilities that I have always naturally performed for women. I can offer business associates car rides home from work that won't be misinterpreted; I can extend invitations that won't be misunderstood to UPS drivers and FedEx deliverymen to come into my home on hot days for cold drinks; I can tutor male college students without fear that the sessions will be viewed as an opportunity for something else. I no longer have to restrain myself from being natural, from being myself. I am now viewed as a nice, maternal, middle-aged woman, and in this respect, I am thrilled.

Now that the threat they once represented is gone, I find that I like men much more. I enjoy their sensibility, their fresh way of looking at things, their intellect, their candor, their humor. Now that I am no longer visible, I am truly being seen by them as a person, a soul. Finally, we can truly be friends.

I understand those women who lament their fading attractiveness to men, and I myself have fingered more than one brochure on plastic surgery. But something positive happens when that thick sexual tension between men and women disappears, and we both begin to see each other for what we truly are—stripped to the essence—human beings. ✿

A Midlife Crisis Celebration

by Debra Johanyak

"Is it warm in here?" My friend Barb fanned herself as she looked around at our 200-plus church members before the service began.

"Uh, I'm kind of warm too," I offered, feeling a slow flush creep into my cheeks. Lifting my church bulletin, my right hand copied Barb's movements in a slow, languid manner that I hoped would not draw attention. Glancing around the large auditorium, I saw several of our cronies in the same posture, sweeping a paper product of some kind to and fro before them.

"Let's ask Mike," I added. In unison Barb and I glanced to my right, where my husband of nearly two decades sat looking forward, eyes half closed, as the soft organ music played.

"It must be us," I whispered to Barb. "His cheeks aren't red yet."

My husband is a good barometer of room temperature. Intolerant of warmth, his light complexion becomes ruddy when the thermometer rises above seventy degrees.

She nodded, looking annoyed at her body's betrayal. Settling into our seats more comfortably, we weathered the sermon, an excellent message about adjusting to life's curve-balls.

"Just what we needed," I smiled as we stood for the altar call.

Making our way to the back of the sanctuary I nearly bumped into Hilda.

"Ooh, my aching shoulder."

"Did you hurt yourself?" I asked in concern.

"No, it's been stiff every morning the past few weeks. It usually loosens up by lunchtime."

Shaking my head, I moved into the hallway to collect my coat from a hanger.

"Hi, Jane. Looking for something?"

My red-haired friend of forty-six stood looking at the coat rack as though deciding which one to buy.

"I came here for a reason, but I already have my coat." She nodded toward the green jacket in her arms.

"Did you leave a dish here from our last ladies' supper?"

"Hmm. No, that's not it." She continued to stare thoughtfully at the coats until her husband appeared beside her.

"Thought you were getting my coat," he teased.

"That's it! I was supposed to get Sam's jacket."

"That happens to me," was my empathetic comment as I headed down the hallway.

Last year it seemed like a dozen or so of the women in our ladies' Bible-study class entered menopause, and we began comparing symptoms each time we met. Soon it was our foremost topic—night sweats, depression, stiffness, forgetfulness, and all the rest of those lovely indicators that our bodies are resigning their child-bearing function.

I had entered perimenopause determined not to let it get in the way of my everyday life, like a quarterback running the ball downfield, pushing past opposing players who try to trip him up. When my mother went through menopause at age forty-seven or forty-eight, I never knew until afterward, when I asked her why she didn't keep pads in the house anymore. She didn't exhibit the classic symptoms that women hear so much about today, or if she did, she kept them to herself. Perhaps that was just as well, since thirty years ago few professionals in the medical or mental health fields addressed the topic of menopause or tried to understand it, much less treat it effectively. I don't recall any of the "older" women whom I personally knew of that generation taking female hormones, though perhaps they were offered and declined. Instead, as in other arenas of female health, women were expected to keep quiet and bear it alone, or in sympathy with each other, without much intervention from the professional realms.

So when I began skipping periods in my early forties, I knew what was coming. I maintained my annual gynecological checkups, kept my doctor apprised of menstrual changes, and when heavy bleeding developed, underwent some tests that revealed fibroid tumors—a benign but potentially serious condition that causes tumors to grow in the uterus. Left unchecked, they can cause heavy monthly bleeding that may lead to anemia. Twice during my midforties I had to take iron supplements when my blood count went too low.

Checking my family history, I found that breast and ovarian cancer run on my mother's side. My grandmother died of breast cancer at age seventy-six, and an aunt developed breast cancer at seventy-eight. Another aunt on the same side of the family was diagnosed with ovarian cancer about twenty-five years ago, but she is now eighty and has been cancer-free for decades. Still another aunt had a breast removed as a young woman because of a suspicious lump, though she died of other causes in her late seventies. In my lateral line, so far, a cousin died of melanoma at age forty-nine, while another survived cervical cancer treated more than twenty years ago. Consequently, I make sure to continue monthly self-exams and annual mammograms for breast cancer. My doctor has prescribed the CA-125 blood test to check for ovarian cancer markers on two or three occasions over the past seven years. Happily I can report that at age fifty, all tests so far are negative. Now I get to line up for a colonoscopy—yippee!

As the weeks passed and I noted that our Sunday morning complaints were increasing rather than diminishing, I decided to do something about it! It's one thing to be uncomfortable for nine months while you bring a new life into the world, but it's another to host uncomfortable symptoms for years with an uncertain "relief point." It was time to become proactive.

Clustering with Anne, an activities coordinator, we came up with the idea of celebrating our unique status as "midlifers" rather than bemoaning it. We would organize a midlife crisis celebration, bringing together facts, food, and fun. We would not let hot flashes and crying jags keep us from supporting each other and pooling decades of life wisdom to pull each other out of the doldrums.

We mailed or hand-distributed fliers to more than fifty women in our church who seemed to fit the bill of "approaching menopause." (I did make one gaffe in handing a flier to a woman of thirty-five—I'd thought she was thirty-eight—who told me in no uncertain terms that she was not at the "target age" yet!) Nearly forty women signed up for our event. Something like thirty-five actually attended what turned into a fun-fest of laughter, reflection, and interaction.

On the night of our get-together, the ladies began arriving as singles or pairs at my house about 6:45, laden with tempting desserts like peanut-butter cream pie and healthy snacks like carrots and dip that would be enjoyed after our gab-fest. I made sure soft drinks and coffee were available all evening. We started with a warm-up activity to test our memories—perhaps not a good idea with our particular group. Anne walked around the circle of ladies with a tray of feminine hygiene items that many of the group probably found quite familiar—tweezers, hair removal cream, and so on—about seventeen in all. Anne allowed each woman to look at the tray for a few seconds before moving to the next person. We covered the tray, then told the women to write down as many as they could remember. We had a couple of ladies who got all but two items, so we gave both of them a prize—a box of designer stationery and a collector's figurine.

Then we got into the "facts" session. We asked each person to share a question or concern about midlife, and the group would offer suggestions or feedback from their own experience. Some had watched talk shows; in fact, Oprah had just hosted a medical professional with a published book about midlife experience, with a list of symptoms to watch for and treat if necessary. Anne shared her Internet research on medical treatments, while I had checked several books about emotional concerns and disorders. One sixty-two-year-old lady described how her moodiness during this time had driven her husband to take up the hobby of golfing so he would be away from the house more. Another woman emphasized the postmenopausal "zest" that brought her renewed vigor and energy. A white-haired participant told us how she lost ten pounds without trying, evidently one of the possible positive effects of moving beyond menopause.

Overall, the exchanges were uplifting and encouraging, leaving us all feeling more informed about what to expect. We also learned something about warning signs, such as unexpected bleeding after you've had no periods for more than a year, or how to avoid bone fractures. We compared experiences with HRT (hormone replacement therapy) and herbal remedies (like black cohosh). We discussed the benefits of regular exercise and stretching routines as well as the emotional rewards of keeping a journal.

One area we did not cover was the financial aspect of the golden years. Statistics tell us that a majority of women will outlive their husbands, yet too many of us still don't know how to balance a bank statement or monitor investments. Some of us don't even know how much life insurance our spouses have, or through which company. So we decided to hold another session to which we may invite informal speakers to inform us about financial investing, for example, or types of life insurance for individualized needs. In fact, our ladies' group is talking about scheduling regular sessions to continue our exploration of the meaning of midlife and the various roles we will be called upon to play, whether it be as grandmother, retiree, innovator, or widow. Hopefully, we also will plan to donate part of our time and experience as mentors and guides, the "wise women" of our age, to help younger women find their paths in life and stay the course.

On Sunday mornings for weeks afterward, Barb, Hilda, Anne, and I—along with countless others—could not pass each other without commenting on our midlife session in excitement.

"Got the next one lined up yet?" Hilda asked at the ladies'-room mirror as we brushed our hair.

"Anne's working on it. She's trying to get her company's financial adviser to come and talk to our group."

"Yay—that would be great!"

Men pride themselves on personal achievement, but women thrive on community. It is through our shared experiences in midlife and elsewhere that we often become healthier, happier, and more productive. I can't wait for our next meeting! 🖋

It's Never Too Late

by Harriet Cooper

I'm never going to be a child prodigy. There, I've said it. The fact that it took me well into my forties and beyond to really believe it proves it's true. The child prodigy boat has most definitely sailed without me. Given the fact that I once got seasick on a waterbed, missing that particular boat may have been a blessing in disguise—at least for the other passengers.

So what am I left with? Shattered dreams? A fear of waterbeds? Hardly a lifetime achievement. And I refuse to look at it that way.

While some people might say I'm a little slow, I prefer to see myself as a lateral thinker. I think outside the box. I color outside the lines. I march to the beat of a different drummer. In short, my glass is neither half full nor half empty. Right now it's lying in the sink because I haven't gotten around to washing it yet. But I will.

Having reluctantly discarded the idea of being a child prodigy—okay, the idea actually discarded me first—I have decided that what I am is a late bloomer. I rather like that word. Bloomer. Someone who blooms. A rose. An orchid.

A chrythan . . . chysan . . . oh heck, a mum. The floral variety, that is, not the other half of dad.

The "late" part of late bloomer is even better because it takes all the pressure off me.

Since my family, friends, and even my cats no longer expect me to do anything even mildly normal, let alone miraculous, I am free to do just that. Perform miracles. I just haven't decided what miracle to perform since so many of the good ones have already been done.

Bringing world peace is probably out of my league, since I can't even get my cats to stop fighting. Discovering penicillin was a good possibility considering what's lurking in my fridge, but that's already been done, so I guess I should really throw out those old containers before they mutate into something deadly. As for making a million on the stock market, well, I bought tech stocks just before they tanked. That pretty much says it all.

Now don't get the wrong impression of me. I am not without accomplishments. Recently, I won an award of excellence from a local charity for my work during their annual fundraising campaign. My moment of glory was short-lived because there was a mixup at the awards ceremony; they had me listed as not attending, so they didn't call my name. But I did get the framed award afterward, and it's sitting on the floor in my office waiting to be hung up.

Someday.

You can come over and see it. You'll just have to move the piles of papers and books that are heaped all over the floor. Actually, that probably explains why my career as a professional organizer never got off the ground. Though I really am better at organizing other people than I am at organizing myself, never mind what my mother says. Yes, mother, I will wash the dishes, do a load of laundry, and vacuum.

Someday.

It's not as if I haven't tried my hand at various careers along the way. I've been a receptionist/typist, a researcher, an office automation analyst, a business analyst, a librarian, a jewelry maker, a picture-frame decorator, an archeologist-in-training, a teaching assistant, and an instructor of English as a second language—to name a few.

I've been good at some, even very good at others, and particularly bad at one or two of them. But the truth is I've never been really great at any of them. Certainly not prodigy level—more of a Bugs Bunny than a Beethoven.

Now, finally, I think I've got it figured out, and it's only taken half a lifetime. But then again, what's a lifetime for if not exploring possibilities, trying new things, taking risks?

What I've finally realized is that I want to be a writer. A humorist. I want to write stuff that will make you laugh and think and then laugh some more. Something that will tickle your funny bone even as it stirs your imagination. And I think I can do it. No, I *know* I can do it. In fact, I'm going to do it.

Today.

So, if you're reading this, and laughing a little or maybe a lot, then look out because you have just witnessed a miracle, or at least the beginning of one: I, Harriet Cooper, am blooming—at long last. ✒

Facelift

by Jerine P. Watson

his problem of growing older is sometimes a *real* problem. Even when one's conscience shakes a shaming finger in your inner mind's face, you wish for the smooth skin of your youth. Especially if you're a woman. And more especially if you're a Southern woman.

I was never a "beauty" by Southern or even Northern standards, but I prided myself on being well groomed. My clothes were not the priciest in high school and college, but I managed to learn how to combine layers and the right jewel colors for a usually successful effect. I like looking "nice" and feeling good about the way I looked. I dealt with the public most of the time, so it was important for me to present a professional appearance. "Dress for success" was the saying in those days.

Time marched along, double-time, then rushing like swirling rapids in a river. Motherhood became my primary profession and my life's priority—for many years. Time left lots of footprints in its heavy-footed way across my life span, and most of those were on my face. I began to daydream while staring at plastic-surgery promos. I could remember pulling up the slack skin on the backs of my own mother's hands and releasing it, watching it settle down into a myriad of little gullies and crevasses, all embellished with ugly brown "liver spots." Now my own hands were replicas of hers.

I spent more time than I care to admit in front of the bathroom mirror, holding the loose skin around my temples back, back, back, and up, up, up, trying to imagine the end result of a masterful surgeon's scalpel. I rather liked the "Oriental look," with my eyes slightly slanted at the corners. I turned my head sideways and thumped the growing wattle under my chin. I pulled my hair back above the hairline and watched my eyebrows rise back up to their original site on my forehead. I smiled without showing any teeth and smoothed back the skin of my now crepe-like cheeks. I even went so far as to take my face in for an estimate, but was deflated beyond belief when I heard the tally for all that I seemed to "need" at this stage of my life. The amount was reminiscent of a lottery win.

I never seemed to have the money for any elective surgery. The nonelective kept eating into my savings, such as extensive dental work, breast cancer, and various and sundry crusty growing things that kept appearing on my skin, not to mention a vacillating blood-pressure reading that required only the most expensive medication. One day I was thirty-three, and the next I was pushing sixty-five. Or so it seemed. But nothing slowed down. On the contrary, my old friend, Time, just whizzed along, faster than ever, and was picking up speed every time I checked.

Not too long ago, I relocated near one of my sons and his family. They are blessed with two children, a girl, four, and a boy, seven. About a week after I moved in, my son asked if I could keep their little girl for the day while he and his wife attended a soccer game with their son. I replied, "Of course!"

since this was the main reason I had wanted to live here, and I was delighted when this blonde Tinkerbelle came bouncing into my small apartment. She loved jumping on my bed and we were gymnasts in our sock feet, singing crazy songs. I told her a long made-up story about the Princess of the Skies (herself) and the Magic Angel who rescued the Princess from the Evil Seagulls Who Ate Children. I had to tell that story over twice more, and each time I worried I'd forget something, but she reminded me of things I'd missed. She didn't forget a word.

Finally, in a fit of giggles, we rolled together in a wonderful hug. She pushed me away and stared into my face with a thoughtful expression. "Bobo, when you smile like that and your cheeks puff out and those wrinkles crunch up your eyes in the corners, well, *that's love*. Didja' know that?"

I wallowed and looked into those clear, blue eyes, with their unwavering conviction of certainty. I held her close and kissed her forehead.

After her father took her home, I went into the bathroom—I have no other mirror here—and stared at my wrinkled face. I turned my face to the side and smiled, watching the starburst of wrinkles crunch up at the corners of my eyes and the "time lines" deepen around my nose and mouth. I recognized the pattern of my own mother's wrinkling on my chin. This time, I didn't push the skin back to simulate the results of a facelift. I touched each wrinkle with my fingers, feeling a new emotion as I regarded the stark evidence of my aging. My granddaughter had seen *love* in my wrinkles, and she was absolutely correct. That was enough of a facelift for me, forever. 🔊

Expressionless in the USA

by L. A. Jasheway

everal years ago, when I first heard someone say they were thinking of having Botox injected into their forehead, what I heard was "I'm thinking of having *buttocks* injected into my forehead." That didn't seem like a good idea at all. I know I'd end up asking all sorts of questions, such as "Does this hairstyle make my rear end look big?" Not to mention how hard it would be to find a hat to fit.

When I discovered that it wasn't buttocks at all, but Botox, a form of botulism that doctors were shooting into patients to paralyze their facial muscles, my natural response was, "Oh, well, that makes *much* more sense!" After all, who doesn't think poison and paralysis are good ideas? Especially when injected just inches away from the brain!

Apparently removing and preventing facial lines is the number-one concern of most American adults. It's higher on the list than paying for schools, finding jobs for the unemployed, or tracking down Osama Bin Laden. In fact, if we ever do find him, some plastic surgeon will probably convince him to have a little work before appearing in court. After all, scowling day after day at Yankee insurgents can create deep forehead furrows, especially in the dry air of a cave.

There's no getting around the fact that we live in a youth-obsessed culture, but can't we just age naturally and get over ourselves? When I see a fifty-something man whose skin is so tight he doesn't dare crack a smile and can't raise his eyebrows, my first thought isn't "Gee, he's young and attractive!" It's more like, "I wonder what would happen if I tickled him mercilessly with a feather? Would his face actually break? And wouldn't it be fun to find out?"

Facial lines say a lot about a person. Without even knowing me, you can take one look at my face and know immediately that I laugh a lot, frown occasionally, and get my makeup tips from circus clowns. A line-free face, on the other hand, says, "Nothing is so important to me that it's worth a facial expression." I have an idea for everyone intent on removing every trace of evidence that they once laughed or cried—pantyhose! A nice pair of pantyhose pulled over your head smoothes out wrinkles, lifts sagging skin, and costs much *much* less than plastic surgery. Plus you can get a tan by simply moving up to a slightly darker shade!

And pantyhose has very few side effects. Just look at the list of things that can possibly go wrong after a Botox injection: bruising, hematoma, drooping eyebrow or eyelid that can last for three to six months (which, coincidentally, is how long it takes until you have to go in for your next injection!), double vision that can last for three to six months, and depletion of your Roth IRA. And you can't drink before having a Botox injection. Hell, how are you supposed to enjoy the hematoma and double vision sober? And if you have Botox treatment for the lines above your upper lips, you probably won't be able to whistle, play a wind instrument, or pucker up for months. But you'll look *mahvelous* and that's what counts, right?

According to one brochure I read while researching this article, the treatment usually lasts only four to six months, unless you are one of those patients who can "break the habit of contracting frown lines and other muscles of facial expression." Perhaps if you get one of those electrical dog collars, you can train yourself out of that nasty habit! (By the way, you should never use one of these collars on a dog. Dogs don't mind having lines and wrinkles.)

I recently saw a news report on three women who had been friends since childhood who all had plastic surgery together. One of them said she was so bothered by the lines on her face that during her commute to work, she spent most of the time looking at her reflection in the rearview mirror and had had a few close calls in traffic. This woman doesn't need Botox, she needs therapy. And a good driver's ed course wouldn't hurt, either.

If the lines on your face are a problem for you, adopt a shar-pei. Just looking at the cute wrinkled face of your new puppy will put things in perspective. And, if it doesn't, you can go ahead and have buttocks injected into your forehead. It's a much better idea than the alternative. ❧

four

New Directions, New Beginnings

It is the soul's duty to be
loyal to its own desires.
It must abandon itself
to its master passion.

~Rebecca West

Baby After Forty

by Jan Andersen

t thirty-nine, I became pregnant on the first try with my partner, Mike, twelve years my junior. I never doubted that I would conceive easily, despite my advancing years. I remember feeling rather proud that all my important parts were still in superb working order.

Imagine then, the horror when I first heard myself referred to as a *geriatric mother.* The three children from my first marriage had been conceived when I was barely twenty-something. Now people seemed to imply that by the time my fourth child had reached school age, I would have a brain like a soggy rusk with the personality and the mobility of a stuffed parrot.

Immediately I scoured the Internet for articles and statistics on birthing over forty. The consensus of medical opinion seemed to be that I was completely past it and was taking a huge risk even *considering* pregnancy at my pre-pensionable age.

Apparently, even if I did succeed in producing a full-term, healthy baby, my tortured pelvic muscles would cause everything to collapse. My bladder and reproductive organs would dangle precariously between my legs evermore. My boobs would probably metamorphose into two flaps of skin, as they had done before, after many months of breastfeeding my previous children, but this time, they would stay flapped.

Despite severe nausea and vomiting, I quickly assumed the appearance of a small hippo. At eight weeks, I could no longer fit into any of my regular clothes. Mike began addressing me with such endearing terms as "Pudding." Lovely. Add this image to heartburn, headaches, abdominal pain due to stretching of the ligaments, and extremely inflated, tender breasts.

Everything around me smelled grotesque, and everything I ate made me sick. I would often sit in the restroom at work communicating with the toilet bowl, thinking I would never make it through another day. On the other hand, all of these symptoms signaled an elevated hormone level and a pregnancy that was definitely here to stay. I welcomed them.

At eleven weeks, I met with my midwife for the first time. Good. She would answer all those awkward questions.

"Ooh, an *older* mum," she cooed, followed by a none-too-reassuring chortle. She began filling out the reams of documentation and noted my date of birth. "You don't look *that* old," she said. Apparently, she was trying to make me feel better.

"*I'm* in my forties," she continued, "and knowing what *I* know, I'd *never* have the courage to have another one at my age," she said, chuckling even more heartily. "If I became pregnant now, it would be a *complete* disaster!" She snorted loudly, her ample chest vibrating.

The midwife merrily cracked jokes about prehistoric mothers as she filled out forms. She took my blood pressure, then checked for the baby's heartbeat, which, she said, she didn't expect to pick up at such an early stage of pregnancy.

"Lie down on the floor, please, dear." She pulled out an electronic device that resembled a thin, white vibrator. She then squirted the obligatory cold gel onto my abdomen. She probed my pubic area a bit too aggressively, commenting on the rather larger size of my abdomen. "Could be twins," she grinned. "You have an increased chance at your age, you know." After more minutes of prodding and further cracking of insensitive jokes, she detected a very definite, very strong heartbeat. Suddenly my baby was real. Suddenly the day was wonderful.

Although Mike accompanied me to my hospital appointment the following week, the casual cruelties of the situation did not improve. It was the first of several visits in which I would have to exercise dexterity in urinating into a two-inch-diameter plastic cup without dribbling over my hands. The scales were placed entirely too close to the waiting room, with the nurse shouting, "You're putting on weight nicely, dear!"

When we finally met our obstetric consultant, he immediately launched into a bulletin of depressing statistics on the chances of a woman over thirty-five conceiving a child with some degree of chromosomal abnormality, such as Down's syndrome. He also talked about the increased risks of miscarriage, pre-eclampsia, pre-term labor, and multiple births. "And will I be able to use my zimmer frame during labor, or would you prefer to use one of those hoists that you attach to elderly people when lifting them out of the bath?" I asked sweetly.

Amniocentesis was duly booked for June 10, four days after my fortieth birthday.

Two weeks and two days later, while I was still lying in bed, Mike came bounding up the stairs brandishing a brown envelope that bore the hospital postmark.

"Shall we open this together?" he asked, launching himself horizontally onto the bed, which created a catapult effect, sending my backside two feet off of the mattress and back down again. *Ufh.*

We huddled together as he ripped open the envelope and unfolded the official white letter. I cannot describe the rush as I read and reread the letter. Our baby had *"no major chromosomal abnormalities."* And our baby was a girl.

I felt slightly triumphant that I had reached nineteen weeks without any significant problems. These results were more proof that age alone doesn't automatically write a woman off.

During the third trimester, when I triumphantly strode into my antenatal appointments, my midwife was as jovial as ever. "Oh, my, rather a lot of glucose in your water. That's three consecutive occasions now. Better make a day ward appointment for you to have a glucose tolerance test. Gestational diabetes can be more common in older mothers, you know," she chortled, delighted to remind me, again, that I was antique.

I didn't have diabetes. Yet another bonus point. Were there any age-related conditions or risks left to throw at me before I delivered my daughter?

"She's still lying with her spine to your spine," said the midwife at my thirty-seven-week appointment, after vigorously pressing around my lower abdomen, then announcing that she had been squashing the baby's cheeks. She shook her head and chuckled to herself while muttering something about a "prolonged, backache labor. Quite prolonged, I'd say." She couldn't stop. "Of course, it *is* your fourth child. *And* there's the age factor," she said. "You realize that because everything's *stretched* and *not as firm* as it used to be, it's more common for the baby to be lying in an awkward position."

At thirty-eight weeks, I went to the hospital for my final appointment with the consultant. While sitting in the waiting area, I bent forward to pick up a magazine. My waters broke.

The especially fashionable hospital wear I was given had missing ties in the back, affording all who cared to look an intimate view of my bum, along with the rest of the action below my waist.

Mike wheeled me into the corridor clutching my inadequately packed hospital bag. My essentials included a packet of fudge, a feng shui book (so I could rearrange the labor room between contractions) and a pair of jeans in anticipation of my body springing back to prepregnancy size within two seconds of the birth. What was I thinking?

After the first half hour in one of the delivery rooms, Mike was high on the anesthetic entinox ("I love this stuff," he slurred, eyes rolling back in his head) while I was hanging over the bed in pain. By midnight, Mike was asleep in the rocking chair, after having consumed the entire bag of fudge; I counted the cracks in the ceiling while pondering my fate.

After a fourteen-hour labor without sleep, I was in a better condition than Mike. He was sporting the 6 A.M. shadow and wearing office attire donned the previous day. He had dark circles under the eyes and was shuffling around like a cripple as a result of having nodded off to sleep in an awkward position. I also believe he was suffering from an overdose of entinox, if that's possible.

Our beautiful, perfect baby daughter, Lauren Erica, emerged at 6:20 A.M. "Two clamps were needed for the baby's cord," the midwife said. "That's the longest and thickest I'd

ever seen. She'd obviously been a very well-nourished baby."
Hah! Another point for the antique!

Life begins at forty, as they say. The second my daughter
was born, my life certainly changed. For the better. Apart from
my breasts, which still enter the room half an hour before the
rest of my body, and an abdomen that resembles a half-set jelly,
all my other vital organs have resumed their original and
rightful positions.

Lauren is now a boisterous seventeen-month-old, with
boundless energy and curiosity for everything except her toys.
My energy levels are higher than they were when I was a mere
twenty-something; my body has eased back, rather than
sprung, into shape. Just now I'm beginning to think how wonderful it would be to give her a baby sister or brother . . . ✑

A New Direction—A New Beginning

by Terri Sherwood Sutherin

I debated for months—even years—about making a change in my life; however, changes, especially major ones, have never been easy for me. I found this particular one to be most difficult because I had such a deep respect and pride for what I had accomplished throughout my life's career. Yet I realized that the restlessness I felt—in my life and my profession—was a problem that only I could correct.

After almost twenty-five years in the classroom, I retired from my position as a high school English teacher, giving me a sense of freedom and newfound energy—both missing from my life for much too long.

Teaching at the same school for the past eighteen years, I thought it possible that I simply needed a geographical change. Assuming a transfer to a new school environment would calm the feelings of discontent within my soul, I asked to be transferred to another high school in our district. This was a new school, less than four years old, and located closer to my home.

In June, I cleaned out my desk, packed up personal belongings, and said goodbye to dear friends and colleagues. I realized that I would be facing new challenges, as any teacher feels—

first-year or experienced—when beginning a new school year in a new building. Also, I was joining an administration and staff with a "youthful and energetic" reputation. I felt confident that this could be the key to regaining my lost sense of joy and excitement about my career and my life.

Being a teacher had filled my spirit with love and compassion; I had "connected" with my students for so many years. It was this honorable profession that had molded me into the person I had become. However, it was also at this time in my life that I found myself struggling with feelings of frustration . . . with dreams of "something more" buried deep inside.

"I cannot ignore these feelings any longer," I explained to my husband. "I've always loved teaching, but now I need to discover new possibilities for my life. I have other career interests, and I really want to pursue them."

"Do what you need to do to be happy," he said. "If teaching is no longer satisfying you, maybe it's time to go in another direction."

However, I was not ready to make such a drastic change. The fear of the unknown still haunted me. And I was afraid that leaving my teaching career completely would be a huge mistake, while relocating to a new school might be the answer I was looking for.

August arrived, and I anxiously prepared for the coming school year. Organizing my classroom to create a feeling of warmth and welcome to those who entered, I attempted to connect with my senior classes from day one. I created new lesson plans, engaging my students to actively participate in their learning process. My renewed enthusiasm was contagious. I truly believed that I could find personal satisfaction and contentment again, if I concentrated on my work and school activities. My deepest hope was to rediscover my purpose in becoming a teacher . . . to make a difference. I knew that I had touched many lives in a positive way over the years, and I wanted, more than anything, to continue to do so now.

Unfortunately, by the middle of September, I realized that I had made a mistake. I longed for that old familiar sense of satisfaction upon waking in the morning, anxious to be the first one on campus and the last one to leave. These were memories of days gone by, days when I eagerly anticipated my students entering the classroom. My classes were fun and challenging; the students were emotionally involved in the lessons we studied, and they easily shared feelings with me in their daily journals, trusting that I would read each one carefully, being empathetic to their individual situations. We were connected through an appreciation for each other. Bonds of respect and friendship were formed that continued to flow through the years, via their siblings and relatives.

The knowledge of what I once had and realization of what I now felt brought me to this critical moment . . . I knew I had to make a decision. My old spark of enthusiasm had dissipated, and it was apparent that the classroom could no longer ignite it for me.

In November, I presented my letter of resignation and retirement to my school principal. She was surprised, of course, but completely understanding of my needs. The weight of the world lifted from my shoulders, and I instinctively knew that this was the right decision for me.

My teaching career ended with the closing of that first semester, just before the holidays in December. I again cleaned out my desk, one final time, packing only a few personal belongings; I left everything (books and supplies that I knew I would never again need) to my replacement teacher for the remainder of the year.

I walked out of my classroom and away from my teaching career, at the age of fifty, with early retirement written across my face—in the form of a smile. With a deep sense of satisfaction, I realized that I was leaving a lifelong career. I had gone full circle to this moment . . . moving in a new direction, excited about a new beginning, and deeply appreciative of the joys that teaching had given me throughout the years.

This was one of the most difficult decisions of my life. As a child, I dreamed of following in my mother's footsteps to become a teacher. Leaving this career, by choice, pulled me in many ways . . . emotionally, financially, spiritually, and physically. Eventually, however, I realized that I must follow my inner spirit, guiding me to reach in new directions.

I finally understood what had happened. Personally, I had changed and grown over the past twenty-five years, and in the process, I lost my passion and now felt disconnected. Struggling with these feelings, I knew that I had to make a change in my life. However, leaving my title of "teacher"— stepping out of my comfort zone—was a huge risk and a serious step for me to take. But I knew I would always wonder, and possibly regret, if I did nothing about the situation.

Finding the strength to identify and value myself—by who I am and not what I do—has been an enlightening experience for me, bringing inner peace and genuine happiness into my life once again. Today, I greet each day with enthusiasm, reaching in new directions, pursuing dreams kept deep inside much too long.

Reflecting on my life since I left the classroom, I find it amazing that the biggest obstacle I needed to overcome . . . was me! I finally understood that it was my duty to take care of myself and that leaving a lifetime career was not synonymous with failure. Creating necessary changes in my life unleashed possibilities that continue to challenge and excite me. Finding the courage to go in new directions has truly awakened my spirit.

As I look forward to the experiences that life offers, I do so with deep feelings of contentment and joy. I cherish the relationships I have with my husband and our two adult children . . . my son happily married, my daughter following in my footsteps as a teacher. I love being able to relax with them now . . . and watch them create their own paths in life.

I now find the time to become involved with my community and develop stronger relationships with friends and family. Knowing that I can volunteer with organizations that are meaningful to me—and create memories with those I love—gives me a true sense of satisfaction and purpose.

I take advantage of opportunities to stay active, taking care of my health and well-being. As women, we tend to put others first—sometimes for years—forgetting that we are only able to give what we have within. Now it's time to make myself a priority.

I start each morning with yoga, or a long walk, enjoying the beauty and peacefulness of nature in the early morning hours; I read great books, and catch up on my many magazines—these used to pile up, one on top of the other, until they became outdated; and I love to explore new places, scheduling adventures with my husband and my father.

Since my mother passed away a few years ago, I think my most significant purpose—and the one that gives me such genuine happiness—is spending quality time with my dad. He lives alone, and at seventy-six years old, has become one of my best friends. Our relationship has found new meaning, and I am so grateful that I have the time to be with him.

I constantly remind myself that I have been very blessed, and I never take a moment—or a day—for granted. At midlife, I finally have come to realize that it's okay to slow down. I plan my days doing what I enjoy most . . . and appreciate every special moment.

Finally, I am able to develop my passions . . . for traveling, writing, and spending time with those I love—most important, me! ❧

The Courage to Try

by Patti Cassidy

*A*nnie stormed into the break room in a huff.

"I won't go back out there!" she steamed. "I've been abused one time too many. I'm almost old enough to retire, and I want to have enough energy left to spend the rest of my life shopping!"

We all laughed. Annie was the registration clerk of our busy ER, and the spring had been brutal. We were understaffed, overworked, and it seemed that everyone in town was sick. Even though we were all cranky, it seemed that Annie could always make us laugh about our problems.

I continued my conversation with Melva at the table.

"I saw this great travelogue about New Zealand last night," I told her. "They showed these people tandem skydiving. They strap your instructor on your back and you both parachute from planes. He does all the work. You just go along for a ride. I'd love to do something like that."

"Patti!" she answered. "I'd be terrified. And besides, you're too old for that stuff. You're forty-seven years old. You'd probably break every bone in your body."

"What are you two talking about?" Annie broke in as she sat with us.

I told her.

"I'd love to do that!" she answered. "When are we going?"

We laughed. But I looked at her and she was serious.

"Seriously?"

"As serious as a snake on a rat," she answered.

We began making plans. My job was to call the skydiving companies in the area to find out if they had tandem jumps and how much they would cost. Annie's was to choose our outfits and make the reservations.

As the day grew closer for our adventure, the rest of the staff looked at us warily. They thought we were crazy. They kept reminding us we weren't kids anymore and that old bones take a long time to heal. The ER docs offered to treat us for free if we had an accident.

We got to the airfield at 2 P.M. The crew there was very helpful, and once we'd watched the safety video, been suited up and instructed, we hit the plane with our instructors. As the small plane climbed toward 11,000 feet, I grew quieter and quieter. As Annie chattered away, I began to wonder what on earth (or *off the earth*) I was doing. I could only think about those awful "falling dreams" I had every once in a while, that woke me up gasping for breath. This jump was sure to be like that. But it had cost over $100, and I was too cheap to waste it.

My instructor patted me on the back.

"One more minute," he shouted. "Let's get buckled up."

"Girl," Annie added. "You're whiter than your sweatshirt."

"One minute," I thought. "One more minute to live. Life is sweeter than I thought."

My instructor hit me on the back one more time and opened the side of the plane. I leaned over and my heart raced. 11,000 feet of thin air. There was *nothing* between me and the ground. And cacti all over the floor of the desert. I was nuts! Everybody was right. I was too old for this kind of adventure!

My foot was on the strut of the plane. My instructor pushed us gently. We were in free fall.

I loved it! I had never felt so free in my life. I weighed nothing and couldn't stop smiling. I felt as if I owned the sky. I never wanted the fall to stop. When my instructor pulled the ring that opened our parachutes, it was a disappointment somehow.

Afterward, Annie and I strutted our newfound celebrity at work. We played up the adventure, letting our stories grow each time we told them. At every opportunity we flashed the pictures that our friend Gil had taken of us as we landed. We were, in short, mighty proud of ourselves.

That skydive was the beginning, and it was a touchstone. I learned that I could be fearless, or at least act that way. The timid girl I was as I grew up, afraid of water, dogs, and high places, somehow faded after the dive, and I took more chances. I grew braver as I grew older. I wasn't frightened of what others thought. I was more curious than I'd ever been about testing my limits. Even though my adventures were tinged with a certain caution (we had, after all, gone *tandem* diving, and not jumped on our own), they opened the world to me.

I made reservations to travel to Paris alone. I took a crash course in French on audiotape, bought two great guidebooks, and had a friend who spoke French well call the hotel for reservations. I chanted to myself, "If I can jump out of an airplane, I can certainly wander the streets of Paris taking pictures."

Another friend begged at the last minute to go with me, since he saw I was serious about taking the plunge myself and it was something he'd always wanted to do. Of course we went and enjoyed almost every minute of our trip.

I applied for a grant to make a short video documentary. I had learned how to use a camera and editing equipment a few years before and was terrified that I'd make a fool of myself. But again I chanted, "If I can jump out of an airplane, I can apply for a grant." And I got it. The video was well received.

A few years later, I knew it was time to relocate cross-country to be closer to my family. I was going to live in the city of my dreams: Boston. I had no firm job commitment and no apartment, though the sister of a friend offered to let me stay at her house while I looked for work. "If I can jump from an airplane, I can move to Boston," I sang on my way cross-country with my cat. I got two job offers the first two days I was in town, and a marvelous apartment across the street from where I worked.

There have been failures, of course. Many things haven't worked out as I'd hoped. But in the trying, and even in the failing, I've grown stronger and maybe just a little bit smarter.

Because of the one time Annie and I jumped out of an airplane, even though we were "too old" to do it, life has changed and grown and become a grand adventure. The fainthearted girl I was growing up has gone and been replaced by a confident, experienced, and open woman who enjoys the world and lives by the motto, "The sky's the limit!" ✇

Reinventing Myself at Forty-Two

by Yitta Halberstam

" *I*f a person hasn't made it by the time they're thirty, they're never going to make it!" My editor at *Seventeen* magazine tossed out these words carelessly one day, dismissively referring to an application from a thirty-nine-year-old whom she was rejecting for a job.

She had no idea how much this cavalier pronouncement would shake me, pierce my psyche like a knife, and haunt me for years to come. As a young, impressionable twenty-two-year-old, I thought this icon—author of eleven books and managing editor of the "special projects" division at *Seventeen*—was invincible, the standard-bearer of Truth. Consequently, I would use her pronouncement as my own personal standard of measurement for close to two decades, and as a result, find myself failing.

It could be said that I had, in fact, peaked at twenty-two. I had been writing and been published since the age of nine, and the pressure to produce was relentless. Perhaps that was why—unconsciously—I chucked the writing life in my late twenties and opened up a dress shop instead. An incongruous choice indeed for someone whose nose was always in a book and whose clothes were perpetually rumpled and out of style. I ended up burying myself in that store, and it took me close to twenty years to reclaim my lost dreams. There were times I was sure it was too late to start over, and my editor's harsh judgmental words continued to ring in my ears. But for me, recovering my old self was not a luxury; it was an issue of sheer survival. I slowly clawed my way out of the pit in which I had entombed myself, one year at a time.

As Jerry Seinfeld might hastily say, "Not that there's anything wrong with being a shopkeeper," but for me, being the proprietor of The Better Half—a plus-size store in Brooklyn—was pure living hell. Each morning when I entered the store I felt my soul falling away from me. I felt diminished and squelched, miserable and unfulfilled. Certainly, I was not using the gifts God had given me, and the work I was doing did not make my heart sing.

One day, my old high school English teacher stepped into the store and looked at me with surprise, followed quickly by sad reproof. "Well!" she muttered, as she surveyed the student voted by her classmates as "Most Likely to Succeed" and "Most Creative." "This is *not* quite how I thought you would end up." I should have been angered by her brusqueness, her tactless words, but shame washed over *me* instead. I bit my lips and simply pretended that I hadn't heard.

Maybe I didn't want to hear. Maybe I didn't want to acknowledge—with the sickening thud that such acknowledgment brought—that the last twenty years had been a waste, a mistake, a terrible squandering of precious time and talent. I could never retrieve those precious years—the years of my young adulthood—when health and energy were abundant, and the possibilities endless. Despair engulfed me as I wondered,

"How have I allowed the parameters of my existence to shrink this way, and abrogate myself to the power of the dollar"—the only real reason I was still in the store? And if I indeed found the courage and wherewithal to finally leave, was there such a thing as a "do-over" for a woman of forty-two?

Somewhere along the line I lost myself,
Somewhere along the line I went off track
Somewhere along the line I left myself behind
And now I'm trying to get myself back.

I wrote the above words in a song when I was thirty-eight, and they became tattooed in my brain, a clarion call for change. I knew I couldn't drift anymore; I had to make a strong effort to re-create myself. And if I failed, at least I would know I had tried and had not simply surrendered to my fate.

I began to work with a therapist. There had been times in my youth when I scorned therapy as a tool for the weak, but by now I was mature enough to know that self-awareness is the first step toward and the prerequisite for change. Then I began to enroll in myriad adult education classes all over the city. It was exhilarating to be in the company of readers and thinkers again, stimulating and exciting to participate in intellectual conversations that went beyond "Bottom line, what's the best price you can give me for this *shamatta*?" Like a tightly closed flower, the petals of my brain began unfurling, and I drank deeply from the wisdom of the people surrounding me. I enrolled simultaneously in a smorgasbord of courses that spoke to my soul—literature, philosophy, religion, psychology—and practical courses that might help me extricate myself from the morass of the store. I alternated variously between classes called "How to Get Published" and "Edwardian and Georgian Literature"; "How to Find a Second Career at Midlife" and "Jungian Archetypes in the Twentieth Century."

In 1991, I finally gathered up my courage and convinced my husband—my business partner—to give me his blessings to seek part-time work in a more stimulating venue, while retaining a strong foothold in the store. We agreed that two or three days a week outside of the store would provide me with the change I desperately needed.

But now that I had my husband's blessing and permission to pursue more fulfilling work, I found I had to contend with the work world itself. Whereas I had been a marketable commodity in my twenties, with stellar publishing credits and youthful energy, now I was no longer a novelty or even marginally interesting to the media world. Where had I been for the last twenty years, everyone wanted to know, and what had I been producing? When I hung my head low and mentioned that I had been a storekeeper, everyone's eyes glazed. "Tell them you started your store from scratch with no prior experience in retail, and that it was a tremendous success," my friends advised. "You showed a lot of initiative, creativity, and talent by creating such a store; the experience has to count for something!" they assured me. But they were wrong. Other stores would have loved to hire me, but no one seeking an editor or writer for their staff gave my resume a second glance.

So, as I was often galvanized to do, I took another course, one on resume-building, which urged an emphasis on "volunteer experience," an area I had ignored. Over the years, I had indeed done a lot of writing—on a volunteer basis—for a local politician who generously gave me an excellent reference. This reference began to open doors previously closed to me.

Ultimately, I was hired as director of special events for a women's nonprofit organization, where my penchant for taking adult-ed classes was parlayed into a stimulating three-day-a-week job that made the rest of the week at the store bearable.

In 1995, I took a life-changing course with success guru Barbara Sher, entitled "How to Be Anything You Want to Be, Even If You Don't Know What It Is!" This three-hour seminar, together with all the previous courses I had taken throughout the years, gave me the last push I needed. Every single one of the courses I took gave me something—even if sometimes it was only a single insight, or one idea, but the confluence of all these courses added up to something significant. Finally, after a sixteen-year chrysalis, a brand-new butterfly—me—was ready to burst out into the world.

Within one month of taking Barbara Sher's course, I wrote a book proposal and sold it to a major publisher. I then embarked upon what I thought would be the long, laborious process of actually writing the work. But hallelujah! There was no laborious process, because the thoughts poured, the words flowed, and sentences coalesced, and a book formed almost magically. When I wrote I felt a certain kind of transcendence, an almost mystical sense of harmony with the universe. But of course, what I was actually experiencing was harmony with myself. I lost track of time when I wrote: Hours sped by in what seemed like minutes, and I lived in a different plane. I felt reborn, renewed, and redeemed. For the first time in seventeen years I felt truly alive.

I only thought there would be this one book. I didn't think that it would in fact launch a brand-new career. But when I typed the last words of the final chapter of this first book, I felt a poignant sadness that the adventure was over. Certainly, I had never felt this way when I closed the doors of my store each evening.

In 1996, I bumped into an old acquaintance, Judith Leventhal, whom I hadn't seen for many years. Engrossed in animated discussion on a sidewalk in Manhattan, we decided to go to lunch, where we continued talking about the power and meaning of coincidence. Judith suggested we try to work together on a book that would look at this subject through a spiritual prism. Our husbands thought we were nuts; the agent who had represented me on the first book thought I was out of my mind. But one publisher—Adams Media—believed in our message and acquired the book.

Judith and I had modest hopes for the book, so we were stunned when *Small Miracles: Extraordinary Coincidences from Everyday Life* catapulted onto all the bestseller charts two weeks after its initial publication in March 1997. Six years, five sequels, and a lifetime later, there are almost 2 million copies of *Small Miracles* in print, and the book has been featured on such television shows as *Oprah, Leeza, Sally Jesse Raphael, It's a Miracle,* and many more. Judith and I still pinch ourselves in gratitude and disbelief. In 1999, my husband and I finally closed The Better Half store after a twenty-year run. I was sure that after all the years, all the emotional and financial investment, all the hopes and dreams that had been pinned onto the store, that it would be a bittersweet experience to finally close it. I did feel terrible for the saleswomen who lost their jobs when we closed, but other than pain for them, there was no remorse. The only regret I had was that we hadn't done it sooner, and that I hadn't stood up for myself long before. I consoled myself with the lesson I had learned from peoples' stories in *Small Miracles:* There is always a reason for everything, even if we can't see the plan ourselves. Perhaps I needed the years at the store to evolve into the person I eventually became (even though I had seen myself as a person in decline). Perhaps I needed the barren, lackluster, unfulfilling years at the store to be able to truly appreciate the opportunities I was blessed with now, in middle age. Perhaps success had come too soon, too easily when I was a child and I hadn't cherished God's gifts enough. Perhaps if all the wonderful things that have come my way in the last six years had come much earlier, they would have meant far less to me than they do today.

And I say with the strongest conviction to anyone reading this essay who has not yet followed their dream or achieved their bliss, it is never too late to start anew. As Barbara Sher so brilliantly says, "It is only too late if you don't start now."

My editor at *Seventeen* magazine is long dead, and I can't personally tell her how preposterous her proposition was: "If a person hasn't made it by the time they're thirty, they're never going to make it!" Grandma Moses was in her seventies when she painted her first picture; Belva Plain was sixty-five when she published her first book; Grace Bloom was eight-six when she earned her master's degree. And exactly how old was Golda Meir when she became prime minister of Israel? If these remarkable women in their seventies and eighties can reinvent their lives, so can you! &

Packing It In

Joyce Maynard

I know people who move every year or two, but I'm the type to hunker down and stay put, myself. I've actually lived in just three houses over the course of my forty-two years. One was my parents' house, where I spent my first eighteen years. One was the house I moved to after leaving college, where I lived on my own for three years and with my husband for the twelve years of our marriage. The third is the house where I live now—bought when that marriage ended seven years ago.

I haven't ventured far afield, either. All three of these houses have been located within a sixty-mile radius of each other, in the state of New Hampshire, where I was born and where I have been raising my own children for the last eighteen years—the last seven of them on my own.

I've made a comfortable nest here for my family and me, surrounded by beloved objects and plants. Just last summer, I painted our house (pink) and put in peonies that won't really get established for another couple of years. I put up a new fence for morning glories. As for the inside—I've remodeled my bathroom and filled my home with yard-sale treasures and large, unwieldy flea market furniture.

For most of my life, I've had an easy time acquiring possessions and a hard time parting with them. Years after my children outgrew their clothes or toys, I couldn't give them away—or a teacup I'd loved, even though the handle had broken off. The way some women find comfort in food, I've found mine in junk collecting, as anybody visiting my house can see. To walk into my living room, you wouldn't guess I'd plan on moving any time in the next fifty years. It looks like a good life we're living here in this place, and it has been.

But though I loved my house, and the easy, comfortable existence we were living in our small New Hampshire town, I started noticing, a year or so back, that a kind of stagnation was setting in. Feeling that your life has a rhythm can be comforting, but mine was starting to feel predictable. Every May I planted tomatoes. Every September I started up at my gym again, and every October my resolve began to fade. Every Christmas I put up a tree in the same spot, spent way too much money on presents, and ended up feeling stressed out and edgy. Every February I fell into a low-level depression from so much cold and dark. Then May came, and I was buying tomato plants again.

But my daughter was graduating from high school in June, and my sons were getting older, too. I went on a book tour, stopping through a dozen cities across the country, and tried to picture us living in them. Suppose we moved to Nashville, and I started writing songs? Suppose we moved to Denver and woke every morning with mountains out the window? What if we lived in Los Angeles, where my sons and I could play tennis year round? And what if, instead of living in a big house with a big yard to maintain, I rented a little condo, or a cabin, or a houseboat?

More and more, what held me back from changing my life had less to do with resistance to change than it did with simple inertia—combined with the daunting task of physically pulling off a move. In the same way that I had once told myself, when I was inhabiting an unhappy marriage, that I couldn't leave because it would simply be too hard to pack everything up, I heard myself thinking, "What would I do with my stuff?" And the minute I realized that it was stuff holding me back, I knew the thing to do was get rid of it.

I wasn't miserable. Not suffering from a broken heart, a job layoff, or a medical disaster. I wasn't moving out of a desire to be with a long-distance lover or move up on the corporate ladder. Mostly I felt a need to grow and a sense that I'd drawn the best nutrients I could out of the soil in my own back yard. What I wanted, for my children as well as myself, was to take in something new. I wanted to look out my window and see mountains and plants whose names I don't know yet, to hear the songs of unfamiliar birds.

I'd also learned—from my last big move, seven years earlier—that the experiences that are the scariest and hardest may also offer the greatest possibility for growth and change. Having moved, once, from a home I loved but had had to leave—when my marriage ended—to a town where I knew nobody, I learned to trust my ability to make a new good home and new friends, wherever I went. Having survived and even flourished in the aftermath of one move, I knew no move would ever be so scary again.

As a person who needs only a quiet room, a desk, a chair, and a place to plug in her computer to earn a living, I possess more freedom than a lot of people do who feel the urge to live someplace new. I also don't have a husband or extended family to hold me down—though, living with three children, I hardly travel light through life. Seeing them game for a move helped, no doubt. I think they recognized before I did that if you don't feel all right about yourself and your life, it won't matter where you move. But when you have a core sense of well-being, you take it wherever you go.

I started asking people (friends, but strangers too) where they'd go if they could live anywhere. A number of people mentioned Seattle, but I didn't want to deal with that much rain, and someone said Colorado, where I knew I'd miss the ocean. When the name of Marin County, California, outside of San Francisco, came up for the fifth or sixth time I figured I should take a look. So I bought myself a cheap airline ticket and flew out for the weekend to investigate. I didn't know a soul in Marin County; I'd never even crossed the Golden Gate Bridge.

I remember the sense of possibility I experienced when I was sixteen, with a brand-new driver's license in my pocket. I felt it when I was eighteen, too, and heading off to college, to a place where hardly anybody knew me, and I knew nobody. I could change my name, dye my hair, take up playing a musical instrument, dispense with my virginity . . . My life was a clean slate. Only for a moment, of course. Then I began filling it up again. And—to a surprising extent—rewriting my same old story.

When we're younger, we get a few chances to start over like that. But it had been a long time since I felt the way I did at the wheel of my red rental car, driving north out of San Francisco to check out a new town where I might want to live.

Usually I listen to music when I drive, but on this particular trip—that first day, and for the four that followed, as I explored Northern California—I didn't want song lyrics and DJ patter to disrupt my experience. I was taking in enough already, just surveying the totally unfamiliar terrain of the countryside and trying to imagine myself in this place.

My friend Patricia, who had made a few big moves of her own, had warned me about the dangers of what she calls "pulling a geographic." Meaning, you make this big, dramatic change in your environment—whether it's renting a new apartment or moving to a whole new part of the country—but fail to change anything within yourself. You tidy up your yard, plant new flowers, and snip away at the crabgrass in your life without uprooting it. And then, of course, the weeds simply spring up again after the very first rain. "Changing hospital beds," another friend called it. Meaning you shift your position on the surface of things. But inside, you still have the same problems you always did.

There's definitely a danger, moving, that all you'll really accomplish is to pull a geographic. But sometimes, too, bringing about a change in physical circumstances can result in some deeper changes. Or maybe it's the opposite I found myself experiencing this winter, when I got the urge to move: Deeper changes had occurred already that made a move possible. When I felt clear that my sense of myself no longer depended on my address or how many dishes I had in my cupboard, I called a Realtor and put our house on the market.

There was something about pulling up in front of our house and seeing a "For Sale" sign in the yard for the first time that made me want to cry, the same as I do when I look at old photographs of my former husband and me, when we were young and in love, or pictures of our children when they were babies. But I also know that just because something was good once doesn't mean you can hold on to it forever, or that it would be good again, if you could somehow get it back. Our house worked well for us, for seven years. The fact that we spent many happy times in this house over the course of the last seven years doesn't mean it would be a good idea, necessarily, to spend seven more years here.

Then the Realtors started bringing prospective buyers through our house. Not yet done letting go, I stayed around too long at first, pointing out special wonderful things about the kitchen and the bathroom they might not have noticed—the Dutch doors leading out to the porch, the special pull-down shelf I'd built to hold a cookbook. I showed them where we put our Christmas tree and told stories about my sons. Finally, gently, the Realtor had to explain to me, "These people need to picture their own family in this house, not yours."

The first actual offer came from a divorced man whose children were grown. His only issue with the house, he said, was where to park his extra-long Lincoln. Maybe he could cut down the lilacs in front, to make a parking space?

I couldn't sleep that night, thinking about our lilac trees, and how my daughter used to wear the blossoms in her hair. When it was time for me to come back with a counteroffer, I refused. "Raise the price," I fumed to the Realtor. "I don't want to sell the house to him."

Then I made another trip to California, with one of my sons. And this time I became a potential home-buyer myself, rather than just a seller. I found a house we loved—smaller, simpler, brighter, with a tiny yard, but a view of mountains and San Francisco Bay out the kitchen window—where I could picture my family and me. My offer on the house was accepted. By the time we got back to New Hampshire, the sight of the "For Sale" sign no longer looked so sad. I knew I had to let go of the idea that I could control what happened in our old house, once it wasn't our house any more.

So—three months from the day I first announced to my family the plan to move, we're packing up the most precious of our belongings and loading them into a small U-Haul for the cross-country trek. We're selling the rest of our stuff at a giant yard sale in a couple of weeks. It doesn't feel so important any more to hold on to every one of my daughter's old dolls or more than one or two baby outfits. I don't need fifteen teapots. One's enough. My friends are not so easily let go, but I don't have to part with them forever just because I'm moving away. A strong friendship with some history behind it isn't dependent on geography.

History, of course, is what's hardest to give up here. I know we'll make new friends in our new house, plant new flowers (container gardening this time), cook good meals, fix up rooms. What you don't have, moving to a new place, are old friends and people who knew you in another lifetime. Because of that, I needed to mark my moving by spending good, relaxed times with the people I love best. I tried to find the right object to give to each of my friends and to do the things we'd always meant but never got around to. I taught my friend Julie how to make pie crust, and she played her flute for me. I took a ride on the back of my friend Joe's motorcycle. I transplanted flowers into my neighbor Lupy's garden.

As much as moving is about shedding the excess baggage, it's also about recognizing which parts of your life are essential, that you need to hold on to. In my case, that means packing up my favorite music, some artwork, my drawing pens and books. Sifting through my mountains of clothes, I realized how few I actually wear, and packed only those.

Sometimes now, lying in bed, among the packing boxes on the eve of our big move, I look around the semidarkness and feel a shiver of pure terror. Where am I going? What will we find there? It's scary not knowing exactly where you're going or what will happen when you get there. Sometimes it feels as if I'm jumping off the edge of the world, not just moving to California.

But the other part, I realize, as I move closer to the day of moving, is what a rare, rich experience this is that we're having. Whenever I tell people what we're doing—moving to a town 3,000 miles away, where I hardly know a soul, the first thing they do is express shock and amazement. The next thing they say is usually, "I wish I could do that myself."

If a person doesn't take risks now and then and reach beyond what's safe and familiar, after all, how can she ever grow? The more you risk, I've learned, the more you stand to gain. It's only when you let go of something you love, maybe, that you'll free your hands to reach out for some good new thing. Moving is about moving away from someplace, of course—maybe a place you loved. But it's also about moving to someplace. Some place you may love even more. 🕭

Granny's Last Cartwheel

by Nancy Harless

amily today is complicated. It hasn't always been this way. Growing up in a small town in the 1950s, my life was so simple. Like all of my friends, I lived in a house with two parents. Mom was there every day when I came home from school, filling our home with cozy smells of something cooking. Dad worked long hours and came home exhausted, but not too weary to watch my tricks when I performed somersaults, handstands, and my favorite of them all, the cartwheel.

He would sit on the porch in the evening trying, I now understand, to have a few moments of solitude. But he would always have a cheer for me as I performed my amazing circus act on the soft green lawn of our front yard. A somersault got a nod; with handstands, he helped me count the seconds I could remain upside down, legs splayed, balanced on those skinny little arms. But it was my cartwheel—my amazing back-arched, legs-perfectly-straight, toes-pointed-to-the-sky cartwheel—that won his applause.

My father found such pleasure in my small performances, unlike his mother, my grandmother. Grandmother was a

201

woman with gray hair who lived halfway across the world in another country called Minnesota. She wasn't fond of noisy children. When she came on the train for a visit, I was reminded that children "should be seen and not heard." My grandmother never saw my cartwheel.

Life then was simple. Everyone knew the rules and knew their role in that choreography we called *family*. But life happens, and with the twists and turns along the way, I grew into my own adulthood and created my own family. By midlife I found that I wasn't only a grandmother to my own children's children, but also to the progeny of my new husband's children as well. Family was no longer simple.

Even the question of "What should they call me?" was complicated because they already had two grandmothers. I dubbed myself Granny Nanny and hoped that it would take. It did. I didn't want to be the granny they feared, whose visits they dreaded. I wanted to be the granny who listened and laughed and loved and played with her grandchildren. In short, I wanted to be a "cool granny."

On one trip to granddaughters Alison and Melissa's home, we visited a beautiful park. It was the very same park where I had often taken my own daughters when they were children. It was here that my children and I had spent many weekends frolicking in the park and, just like with my own childhood productions, they would run and skip and jump and somersault with glee shouting, "Watch me! Watch me, Mommy!" and then I would join them and amaze them with my perfect, back-arched, legs-straight-toes-pointed-to-the-sky cartwheel.

On this sunny summer day, Alison and Melissa were bursting with the joy of youth. They began to run and jump and amaze us all with the gymnastic feats they could accomplish.

No mere somersaults or cartwheels for these two young gymnasts. They twisted and whirled with back flips, round-offs, and amazing multiple cartwheels. I applauded in awe.

When they paused to rest and walked back toward me, I couldn't resist. I knew better, or should have at least, but I was caught up with the excitement of the show. "I can do an amazing perfect cartwheel," I announced. Both girls grinned at each other as if to say, "Granny? A cartwheel? I don't think so." Melissa even snickered.

So I accepted the challenge. The sun was bright, the sky was filled with puffy cumulus clouds, and there was just a little breeze. In the distance, birds could be heard calling to each other. I inhaled deeply and, with a drum roll playing in my head, began the running skip that introduced my cartwheel. Arms raised overhead, I catapulted heels over head with my back arched, legs perfectly straight, toes pointed to the sky. I was flying!

I was also in pain! The centrifugal force of the circular spin of the cartwheel became too much for my middle-aged joints. With a loud CRACK my left leg, the trailing one, came out of its socket in my hip. Next, as I ended my circular descent, both arms raised overhead—the way you always end the show—my left leg was slammed back into its socket with a dull thud. The pain! Oh the pain! But not wanting to frighten the children, I blinked back my tears.

"Wow, Granny, you really can do a cartwheel!" Alison exclaimed as Melissa beamed widely at me with a newfound respect for her Granny. I vaguely remember mumbling something about how we should always warm up before exercising and that Granny had forgotten to do it that day.

The next morning, my husband had to help me get out of bed. Every joint in my body ached with a vengeance. Warmed up or not, I knew that yesterday had taught me something: That was Granny's last cartwheel!

Yes, family today is complicated, but I can still come to visit all of my grandchildren, those related to me through blood or by marriage, and be called Granny Nanny. We can still listen and laugh and love and play together because, be it through shared DNA or through a shared history, that is what family does.

On a day in the park, the sun was bright, the sky was filled with puffy white clouds, and in the distance I heard the birds call to each other. A soft breeze blew, just enough, and for one brief moment in time I soared, back arched, legs perfectly straight, toes pointed to the sky, performing Granny's last cartwheel for my granddaughters' pleasure. And they knew that their Granny was cool. 🐚

I Was a Midlife Motorcycle Chick

by SuzAnne C. Cole

here's a black plastic helmet six inches in front of my face. Beside this dome, over the driver's shoulders, I see tan forearms, blond hairs glinting in the sunlight, and hands clutching black rubber grips. When I turn my head slightly to the right, I see my helmet-encased chin in the rearview mirror and, below us, the gravel shoulder whisking by.

I am on my first-ever motorcycle ride, courtesy of our upstairs neighbor in the condo complex in New Braunfels, where we have our vacation home. As we chatted with him last night after we arrived for my birthday weekend, he mentioned buying himself a motorcycle to celebrate a change in career. Instantly an adolescent self, slumbering since she'd been told nice girls didn't ride motorcycles, sprang to life and exclaimed, somewhat to my horror, "I want a ride." Twenty minutes ago, I answered the phone and heard Billy say, "Put on your long pants, girl, and let's cruise."

Abandoning the bed where I had almost put myself to sleep reading a *New Yorker* profile of a classical pianist, I pulled on a pair of camping pants and hurried out to see my chevalier dusting off his black Suzuki. Then he offered me an astonishingly heavy helmet. Putting it on, I felt encased and isolated, so I joked off my anxiety by raising my arm and intoning, "May the force be with you." He showed me where to put my feet, and his wife suggested I hold on by hooking my fingers into his belt loops. (And that's what I did, but if we were intimate, I think I would be hugging his hips with my thighs, leaning as he leaned, feeling the road through both our bodies.)

My husband took photos, Billy revved the engine, and we were off. I had assumed we would loop through the condo/housing complex once or twice and that would be my ride, but instead we headed straight for the highway. At the intersection, Billy asked if I wanted to ride up to Canyon Lake or down to the town. "Oh, the lake," my adolescent daredevil instantly responded, and away we went on Highway 46, a small black stone in the stream of Labor Day traffic.

With no way to be in control, I start to relax. I can't even see where we're going, but I can swing my heavy head cautiously from side to side and glance at the landscape. Individual mesquite bushes and stands of cacti register in sharp relief as we speed past. I feel the road vibrating through my bottom and risk loosening one hand from Billy's belt loops to rest it on my knee.

A brief wave of guilt washes over me as I remember how inflexible my husband and I were when our three sons begged for motorcycles—no, absolutely not, not negotiable, not while you're under our roof. All I knew then of motorcycles was my younger brother's experience. On his first day of ownership, he motored past a stalled car, failed to look for oncoming traffic, was hit by a car, and got propelled into a ditch. Not badly hurt, he limped home pushing the damaged cycle, which our parents insisted be sold the same day. Shaken by the incident, he didn't protest, and motorcycles were never again part of our adolescence.

I never knew this side of riding, sun shining on my neck and shoulders, shirt billowing in the air, tasting the breeze, feeling part and particle of the landscape we pass. Is it too late to tell the boys—now well into adulthood—that their mother regrets her obduracy, and if they can find a driver as trustworthy as I have, they have my permission to ride?

We reach Canyon Lake and another decision—return to the ranch on the highway or take the river road? "Oh, the river road, please." It's rained all week in New Braunfels; the Guadalupe, clouded with mud, flows quick and green. I wave shyly at the motorcyclists and their women we meet on the road. I'm on the road, too! I can't stop grinning. Speeding on the straightaways, slowing to negotiate curves and cross the river, we are treated with surprising courtesy and respect by cars. Ten miles of river road, and then we're on the highway heading back to our condos. Perhaps it's time; my bottom aches from the narrow seat.

As we approach the entrance to the ranch, Billy pumps his bent arm and I echo the movement. I am proud of my ride; I only wish we'd seen somebody I know. I understand now why motorcyclists resent the helmet law. Heavy (my neck aches from holding my head upright) and hot, the helmet has restricted my view, prevented me from fully feeling the wind in my face—and it has kept people from recognizing me.

Arriving back at the condo, I thank Billy profusely for my most adventurous fifty-fifth birthday experience and slide stiffly off the seat, feeling as I do so, a quick spark of intense warmth on my leg as I apparently brush against the hot muffler. He doesn't notice and I say nothing. He says graciously that cruising in company is always more fun.

Walking into the condo, I discover two burn holes at the bottom of my new camping trousers and a spot of melted fabric on my socks. Thick socks, however, have prevented all but the very slightest of burns, a badge of honor, a symbol of my new risk-taking midlife self. Three weeks ago, I, who had never camped before, backpacked five miles into the Sierra Nevadas with seven women for five days, spending one day and night utterly alone. Now I've ridden a motorcycle. What's next? Would it be too painful to get a tattoo? 🐌

Old Dogs, New Tricks

by Midge Crockett

They say "Life begins at forty," and I'm a good listener. Consequently, I felt cheated on my fortieth birthday when it appeared that nothing was beginning for me. Particularly life. So, I began singing the "Poor, Poor, Pitiful Me Blues." But eight years later I was whistling a different tune. In 1997, I was within a month of turning forty-nine, had celebrated twenty-five wedding anniversaries, raised two kids, two husbands, three dogs, two cats, a cockatiel, and Pete the hamster. With the exception of one husband, none of the aforementioned needed me any longer. For the first time, I took the bull by the horns and decided what to do when I grew up. Fascinated by the power and complexity of words, I decided to pursue a degree in English. I wanted to try my hand at writing. After enrolling at Wenatchee Valley College in Eastern Washington, I applied for a federal student loan and signed up for my first twenty credits—four periods a day. Plotting out the prerequisites for an associate of arts degree, I signed up for English, math, psych, and biology. My college courses turned out to be the last regular periods I would ever again experience! Not only did I find myself in the Halls of Education but, also, in the throes of menopause. I entered the "Night Classes, Hot Flashes" zone, and life began at forty-nine.

Spring quarter commenced on April 7, 1997, accompanied by a change of life. That evening, laden with anticipation and textbooks, I gingerly pressed my right hip against the chrome latch bar on the door nearest the student lounge. Behind this door, a new world of understanding and enlightenment was waiting for me. As the door gave way for me, there it was—the college cafeteria. Undaunted, I referred to the campus directory at hand and located the correct door. The one leading to the main hallway and the classrooms.

The classroom environment was actually very exciting, and I felt at ease in the hallowed halls of academia. Interestingly, learning and concentration came much easier than they had back at West Seattle High School, class of '66. Thirty-plus years ago, I didn't look much further than beyond the tip of my nose and didn't appreciate higher education. I don't recall that I ever strained a brain cell in the pursuit of a particular curriculum— except maybe Boy-Watching 101 and Gossip II. My impetus for finishing high school and maintaining passable grades was simple: My parents assured me that going to school was good for my health because it guaranteed my nether region would remain intact. Back then, any thoughts I entertained about attending college couldn't hold a candle to my grandiose dreams of love and marriage and a baby carriage. Once on the wrong side of forty, though, I developed a kind of if-you-don't-use-it-you-lose-it attitude about brain muscles. Fortunately, my brain saw the need for a bigger challenge than reading the *TV Guide*. Attending college was a sensible solution.

At my halfway-up-the-upward-side-of-a-downward-slope age I wasn't sure that I would blend with a crowd of callow collegians. I had a skewed slant about age when I was an undiscerning teenager. Mr. Wesley Smyth, my tenth-grade science teacher, was a genuine relic. A nice enough guy, but rather old-fashioned; I imagined that being his age must be a real downer. One day, while lecturing the class on the principles of science-type stuff, "Old Man Smyth" let the year of his birth slip. A brilliantly quick calculation revealed that he was—Oh, dear Lord!—thirty-seven years old. My bet was these kids would have me figured for Methuselah. Me, the newest kid on the block and the oldest kid in my class. An amusing thought. However, with my new, middle-aged mental set, I wasn't uptight about other people's views. It pleased me no end to find that classmates considered me a mentor, and faculty related to me as a peer.

Most of the professors were, in fact, somewhere in their middle ages, except for Mr. McIntyre, a biology instructor, who was my junior by a bit more than a score. The majority of the student body was in their late teens. One of my classmates, Tonya—a self-proclaimed "professional student"—had recently struck the big two-five. Interestingly, my age became a positive communications factor in understanding the world around and within me. The instructors and I shared mutual respect and admiration as we spoke freely about our home and family lives. Walking, talking, and dining with classmates five days a week provided a welcome chance to confront and accept our diversity and to celebrate and embrace our uniformity. Classmates began seeking my advice on scholastic and personal matters, opening wide a door of comfortable communication. Because I was the Grande Dame and naturally attributed my acquired skills and varied experiences to age, my classmates, bless their hearts, thought that instead of being saggy and wide, I was sage and wise. In some ways, though, I was as young as they. And they were as old as I.

As classes continued into the first semester, I began to realize the irrelevance of age and believed what mattered is how you *feel* about age. While teaching a topic on human development, Michael "the kid" McIntyre separated our class into groups of four students each. He assigned us the project of selecting, researching, and speaking on any element of physical and/or emotional development common to mankind. We had a week to prepare. My group was assigned to prepare a montage of different ages and perspectives. Needless to say, I was the senior member of the group, which also comprised Rachel, Geremy, and Tyler.

Rachel was a somewhat timid, very bright, slightly plump, fifteen-and-three-quarter-year-old high-school junior who attended the college through the governmentally funded preparatory program called Running Start. Geremy (yes, with a *G*), appearing much younger than his eighteen years, was a polite, lanky, crew-cut class clown whose *raison d'etre* for higher education was, "It keeps my mom and stepdad from kicking me out of the house." Tyler, the second oldest of our group at just-turned twenty years, had gorgeous sandy-blond hair and deep blue eyes. He was a hunk of muscle working on his B.A. in Standing Around and Looking Good. And then there was me.

After reviewing and discussing the class notes, three-quarters of the group agreed on a verdict that "Psychological and Physical Aspects of Puberty" was a wise choice for research, and it would likely cinch an "A" from McIntyre. Unfortunately, I figured I couldn't contribute much on the subject—not from experience anyway—so I was the lone holdout on a hung jury. Hardly remembering how to pronounce "puberty," let alone recall its aspects, I suddenly felt overripe. A prune of a woman embarking on menopause.

The kids were intuitive and sensed that I wasn't elated with their choice of research subjects. "How about Psychological and Physical Aspects of Age?" Rachel suggested. The proposal to research the aspects of both puberty and menopause was politically sound and passed unanimously. We soon discovered that all the years between their puberty and my menopause didn't amount to a hill of beans.

By the third day of the biology assignment, we were having a grand time disclosing certain personal details about our life changes. Hours spent on campus library and Internet research began paying off and pointed us in the direction of self-discovery. Amazingly, the more I learned about puberty and its similarities to my newly found menopause, the better I understood that the wonders of youth and middle age should be shared and discussed openly. One of the reservations I held about menopause—other than seeing my naked body in a mirror—was about growing old. As Rachel, Geremy, and Tyler separated the fallacies from the realities of puberty, they came to grips with their uncertainties about growing up. Contrary to the old saying, ignorance is *not* bliss and familiarity does *not* breed contempt. By the end of the week, our report was prepared.

During menopause and puberty, emotional and physical changes are the byproducts of the same basic phenomena— wild and wacky hormones. In puberty, right about the time a child begins to revolt against everything parental, armies of untrained hormones—hordes of newly enlisted progesterones, estrogens, and testosterones—break camp and start marching through our bloodstream. Having no one to lead the way, these disoriented hormones wreak unfettered havoc on their newly invaded territories. Our group began referring to puberty as "The War of Rebellion." Three or four decades later, these same vast armies, who have learned to parade in orderly fashion while carrying out their duties, begin to notice their troops dwindling. And everyone knows that there is nothing more devastating than a dwindling troop. So, as the hormones continue ebbing, the commanding gland issues an urgent message and the remaining troops panic. Another conflict breaks out when the hormones fight for their lives as they are urged from our bloodstream. Welcome to menopause, or as our group called it, "The Battle of the Bulge."

War is Hell. Despite thirty or forty years between the onset of these two skirmishes, and considering that puberty and menopause are at opposite ends of the spectrum, the resulting battle scars left by each are analogous. Rachel confided in me that she was only about two years into her pubescent development and was worried about being a "late bloomer."

As the discussions continued, I remembered puberty's effect on me. It seemed like a hundred years ago that my unpredictable hormone levels prompted parts of my body to simply start popping up. Breasts, body and pubic hair, hips, growth spurts, body odor, and pimples seemed to just appear out of nowhere at the most inopportune times. Budding breasts grew larger, the waistline receded, hips curved, body hair sprouted, fluids excreted, and emotions ran amok. And I was left with a brain that was, at that time, a patty short of a Big Mac, to manage and make decisions for my adult body. No wonder puberty is such a confusing time.

Confusion revisited in 1997. After enjoying a symbiotic existence for nearly thirty-one years, my hormones were threatened by menopause and went bananas. They incited conditions akin to puberty. This time around, though, my breasts grew not so much larger as longer; the waistline didn't recede, but advanced; hips deviated more than curved; hair began to sprout on my chin and upper lip; and every now and again, a third eye appeared on my forehead. (Clearasil still works, by the way.) And talk about fluid excretions. My best friend told me once that ladies don't sweat . . . only *men* sweat. Ladies "glisten." She was so wrong. During menopause I didn't glisten, nor did I perspire. Didn't even sweat. I lathered up like an out-of-shape racehorse. About three times a day, I feel partially responsible for global warming because my hot flashes emitted thousands and thousands of BTUs into the atmosphere daily for nearly two years. No wonder menopause is such a confusing time.

Menopause, confusion, and my college experience are behind me now. With help from Rachel, Geremy, and Tyler, I made it through college with flying colors. The four of us, despite our differences, truthfully shared our failures, our uncertainties, our successes, our shoulders and, most important, our ears at a time when we needed to be heard. Rachel is now interning at the University of Washington Medical School and Hospital in Seattle. She and I stay in touch by e-mail, although not as often as we'd like. She recently thanked me in a long letter for "being there" through the toughest part of her change of life. She is doing well and said her hormones are behaving like little ladies. Her periods are regular. Adding that she knows better what to expect in her next change of life, shy little Rachel made a funny observation. "It's not that I'm looking forward to middle age," she wrote, "but it'll be great not having to go with the flow!"

An English degree was the least of my rewards for going to college. College is where I learned so many things. Most important, college lit a fire under my rear that urged me to begin my life. All the snippets of wisdom I learned from my classmates about their life changes and my life changes helped me build stronger relationships with my grandchildren. Four of them are experiencing life changes, and there are six more kids to go. They know I understand now. I forgot what being a child was like. I forgot how sane it is to open up. I forgot how important it is to listen. Now, my grandchildren should know that I will be at their beck and call with an open ear. My college friends and instructors helped me remember the important things. That's a great reward.

Now, at fifty-five, I have a wonderful routine, yet I'm not stuck in a rut. I know what works and what doesn't. If it doesn't work, I can fix it. If I can't fix it, I know who can. The value of my English degree is immeasurable. It reminds me that it is never too late to learn. You can teach an old dog a brand-new trick. 🙠

The Acid Test

by Mary Terzian

I could barely see a yard ahead as I drove in the pouring rain to a writing class at UCLA, half a century late. The tapes engraved on my left brain were turned on full blast.

"What are you doing? Who do you think you are to write memoirs? At your age you should be sitting by the fire, knitting."

By the time I found parking, the building, and the room, I was half an hour late. I walked in, drenched to the bones, parading my defeat all the way to the front corner of the class, the only seat available under the professor's nose. No, she didn't have a big nose, nor was she the literary giant I expected. She had a cute face and a tiny frame lost underneath a jungle of hair. She was like a spring ready to pop loose from her high chair any minute, nothing like your run-of-the-mill, bespectacled, age-old erudite professors who sport their white beards as proof of their wisdom. She had a sharp wit, though.

"What's your name?" she asked and made a point to account for my presence.

I looked around. What was I doing among these kids? The bright twenty-year-old in the first row particularly unnerved me. I could be her grandma!

The professor rambled on for a while. All I could hear was "what to put in, what to leave out." Easy to say. These young adults had not lived yet. I had a whole lifetime to squeeze into thirty pages. The account of any five-year period of my life would be longer than that.

"Before I put you to sleep, let's have some fun," the professor roared to the class. "Get your pens and paper ready." Everybody's interest was piqued.

"We're going to have a fun exercise for ten minutes." She held up a brown bag for all of us to see. "I will pass this bag around. Don't look in it, but grab an item and write about it from your stream of consciousness, whatever it reminds you of. This is just a warm-up exercise to strengthen your memory. Don't expect a masterpiece, and don't edit please, let it flow. Nobody is going to read it except you. Wait till everybody has picked an item."

One by one we drew something: a comb, a logo, a key; of all things, I picked a lemon.

"Does everybody have an item? Okay! Start!"

What could be exciting about my item? I pondered for a while. As time went by, under the teacher's raised eyebrows, I became nervous. Was she considering me a failure already? "A senior! What is she doing here occupying valuable space? If she starts her memoirs now, when will she finish?" I banned those negative thoughts from my mind for a more productive exercise.

"I picked out a lemon," I wrote. "What else! This is the story of my life. I always end up with lemons."

"When I was young I loved sucking on lemons. I dipped them in salt to further enjoy their acidity. I wish I had not. Those lemons soured the future course of my life. I wish I had dipped my fingers in jam.

"The first lemon was my 'Simca,' the car I owned in Togo. I was transferred a month after I acquired it.

"The second lemon I picked was my husband. Needless to say, the marriage didn't last long, but it provided me with the life-long custody of a child.

"My third lemon was my Vega in Los Angeles. It guzzled gas, broke down a lot, and was totaled at 40,000 miles . . ."

I continued in the same vein, putting all my lemons in one basket, throwing in a job for good measure and a boss for dramatic effect. It was a catharsis of sorts, squeezing out from my own system all the frustrations piled up in a lifetime. Actually, it was fun. In my own way I was getting even.

"You have one more minute," announced the teacher, "wind it up."

I wrote the last paragraph:

"I have a nose for picking up lemons," and then elaborated on the "do's and don'ts of avoiding the acid test."

"Stop!"

We put our pens down.

"Now," said the professor, "I want a few volunteers to read what they wrote." This didn't strike me as fair. She had said nobody would read our writing except ourselves.

In the absence of hands showing, the teacher concentrated her stare at me, since I was the closest to the lectern—or was it age discrimination?

"Will you volunteer, Mary?"

Did I pick a lemon of a class too? My stream of conscious-ness was not meant for public exposure. I was mortified to read the story of my life to these young students, who probably did not have anything in common with me. Had I known ahead of time, I would have held back some unpleasant details. Why corrode their lives with my "acid experience"?

I grew crimson with each sentence. I heard a few chuckles. Were they amused or laughing at me? I played hard at keeping my composure. The professor went on to others. She then elab-orated on the use of wit and humor in recalling memories. I sat there quietly, planning an honorable exit as soon as the class was over. Instead, I found myself squeezed between two stu-dents at the door.

"I loved your lemons," said one guy, a reporter for a major paper.

"You sure have a lot of juice," butted in another. "Hey, that was witty. I want to know more about it."

My self-confidence climbed a few inches. Their comments provided me with enough nerve to return the following week. It felt good to be among the younger folk.

"How's your lemonade, Mary?" yelled a student from across the hall, as I made my way in to our second session.

"As tart as it can be," I yelled back.

I had passed the test. I was one of them. Age didn't matter anymore.

It was the best lesson I learned in that class.   🦋

Fallen Leaf

by Jeri Ledbetter

inter has pulled a blanket of snow over the mountains and foothills of northern Arizona, asserting its arrival. Besieged by prolonged drought, the thirsty trees embrace the precious gift; they have caught as much of the snow in their outstretched limbs as they can hold. Perched on an old lava flow born of the dormant volcanoes to the north, a small wooden house protects the woman inside—me—from the cold morning air.

Sitting by a window, I hold down a chair, desperately trying to coerce words into sentences. I am following the advice of a friend—a gifted writer—who said, "The secret to writing is keeping your butt in the chair."

Well, perhaps there's more to it than that. I sigh, forgive the unfocused words that taunt me from the monitor, and look out the window at a dazzling scene of unbelievable white, accented by ponderosa pine and scrub oak trees that march up the hill behind the house. Only the snowy feet of the distant trees are visible, unless I move from my chair . . .

"Don't do it. Just sit here." My stern command to myself alarms the cat, who jumps down from a nearby chair, glares at me, and huffs toward another room. "Sorry." His tail twitches angrily. I am clearly unforgiven.

Just outside the window, three acorn woodpeckers demand my attention. One swoops in, lands on an oak tree, and strikes it with his bill a few times, closing his eyes as beak hits wood. Then he squawks at his companions, his black, white, red, and yellow clown-face turned sideways. Answering the invitation, another flies in, landing just below to join in the hammering.

Drilling holes into trees with one's face seems like a tough way to earn a living, but woodpeckers must be well designed for such abuse, or they would have joined the list of extinct evolutionary experiments that were simply too ridiculous to work out.

Perhaps I should have listened to the advice of another writer: "Design a workplace with no windows; board them up if you must." I never considered it a serious option. I have spent too much time outside, with gentle wind caressing my hair and bold sky providing my ceiling, to voluntarily confine myself to a box.

I force my eyes back to the computer screen, while the clowns cackle, swoop, and undermine my futile attempts to concentrate. A flash of black, yellow, white, and impossible red flaps past and disappears outside the window. The bird drills into the siding of the house above my head.

"Hilarious."

I turn to watch again. Their antics interrupt, but they fill me with joy. The bird flies back to an oak tree, just outside the window, landing on a snow-covered branch stripped bare by the hardness of winter of all but one brittle leaf. My eyes widen with a strong memory. I laugh and sit back in my chair. "What, this again? I thought we worked through this a year ago."

My hands still rest on the keyboard, as though keeping them there will force words to appear on the nearly empty computer screen. Then I move them to my lap, resigned to the memory that barges into my mind. My thick, wrinkled hands tell a story of someone who has worked hard outside—out of passion rather than necessity. My lined face reflects the same— long days of unrelenting desert sun have left their mark. My short hair is still mostly blonde, with gray hints of middle age and all that goes with it. I look at the single leaf, smile softly, and remember the previous year.

The wind had screamed for days when it delivered fall to the desert mountain. Battered leaves lost purchase and settled onto the ground, and began the next phase of their existence— nurturing the trees from which they fell. Most leaves, anyway. Always a few remained for an unbelievably long time, relent- lessly clinging by brittle fibers, refusing to give in to the inevitable.

It was late November. Sleet tapped the window to advise me of the coming winter, but I was well aware of its advent. I watched in comfort out the window of my warm, quiet home as the outside world raged with the change of seasons. An acorn woodpecker rushed from tree to ground to tree, franti- cally hedging his bets, preparing for the hard days to come. Now and then he swooped in and pounded his beak at the seed bell I hung to entice birds into a visit. I had been watching the oak tree just outside my window these past weeks, as one by one the leaves relented and fell. This day, only one remained.

"Give it up, already," I had told the leaf through dirty glass. "Stop this silliness of clinging when you know what needs to happen. What are you so afraid of?"

My own words alarmed me, my concern having little to do with the obvious—that a middle-aged woman was initiating a philosophical conversation with a leaf.

My marriage was ending. Over the past few months I had watched helplessly, unable to stop irrevocable change in my world. The harder I tried to hold on, the more it slipped through my fingers. My husband was trying to choose between a life with me and a life with someone more intriguing. A codependency poster boy, he seemed incapable of making up his mind. Meanwhile, I twisted painfully in the breeze.

"Okay, leaf. What's it going to be? Must we decide for him?"

The discussion went on for several days—with the leaf, and with my friends.

Gut-wrenching was not new to me. Fifteen years earlier, after a decade of marriage with a man who could not be consistently kind, I had fled from his angry words and volatile temper. Struggling to make it work, trying to believe he could change, then attempting to adapt to a life and a relationship that didn't fit, I had waited too long before I finally escaped. I landed hard, like I'd fallen off a cliff.

Lost, alone, and desperately sad, I happened to land among the people who run boats through the Grand Canyon—misfits, geniuses, and lunatics, drunk on adrenaline and crazed with attention deficit disorder.

The Colorado River, which etched the Grand Canyon a mile deep into the earth, offered quiet reflection in a stunning pageant of rock, water, and life. Resilient life so vital in the desert surrounded, nurtured, and reassured me. The people who spent much of their lives floating the river, exploring the vast fullness of the canyon, and sleeping beneath the stars with their view obscured by its walls, offered comfort and accept-ance. For the first time in many years, I felt at home; I wanted to be a part of this community. But first I had to learn how to row a boat.

During the last ten years of my former life, I had run a property management business. My manicured nails, soft, white hands, and 115-pound body unaccustomed to physical work failed to inspire faith in my new companions. Could this wimpy creature row boats through heavy whitewater? Their reservations were not unwarranted. Later, my mentors would recall the hilarious and lengthy training process during which, they admitted, they brought me along for "comic relief." On my first trip rowing a raft, I proved not that I could row, but rather that I could endure a series of beatings and humiliations, and still not give up.

These kind people embraced me without reservation, taught me what they could, and put me back in my boat, breathless and confused, when a wave occasionally sent me flying into the river. A few of the men welcomed me with open legs as well as arms, but perhaps I needed that at the time. For a while, I fell in love with any man who would be kind. Eventually I realized that a lot of men would be kind. Desiring only one, I raised the bar a bit. Yet at any hint of anger or unkind words, I would bolt.

There was this guy, a boatman, who wore goofy clothes, rarely bathed, sporadically brushed his hair, and never seemed to get angry. He told wonderful stories of life on the river, was charismatic and intelligent yet humble, and I didn't give him a second glance for some time. Later—much later—I realized that I had known from the beginning that I could never be enough for him.

But he turned to me, and I melted into his eyes, his body, his life. I came to love him deeply, yet felt there was a part of him he would not allow me to touch. There was a sadness in him—a quiet desperation—and a fierce sensitivity that so threatened to devour him that he could not allow himself to feel too much. Still knowing I could never be enough, I tried to be. He never did yell. He remained incapable of unkind words, but his was a soul more tortured than mine. Emotional cripples, we spent the next fifteen years muting our emotions. Over the past few years I pretended to my river family, to myself, and to him that all was well.

The dam finally burst. Afraid, apologetic, an emotional puddle once again, I sought counsel and sympathy from my friends. My marriage, I admitted, was a wreck. They were appropriately empathetic and disturbingly unsurprised. This was no revelation. Perhaps they had been simply waiting for me to figure it out.

Once the words were said, more spilled out behind them, spreading across the floor like a flood. And, for the first time, what I feared most became real. And survivable. My friends did offer advice, along with love and acceptance that washed over me and gave me strength. They told me to be kind to myself. "Take good care of yourself. You will survive this." Again and again they told me that they loved me.

I embraced my friends, and they held me close. I focused my attention on my life, rather than his, or our lives together. I realized, for the first time in many years, how full and rich was my own existence. How had I lost sight of that? I learned to accept myself, as Jeri, rather than as Jeri-and-him. I began to seek what life expected of me, rather than the other way around. I wrote like a crazy woman, releasing previously guarded thoughts and emotions, occasionally looking out the window to watch the acorn woodpeckers, and to laugh.

I opened my mind, and moments of enlightenment made me dizzy. Victor Frankl, a psychiatrist who survived imprisonment at Auschwitz, maintained the last of human freedoms that cannot be taken away—to choose one's attitude at any given moment, to find meaning in one's existence even under the most dire and hopeless conditions. This freedom can't be denied—not to the most helpless victim. Yet as volunteers, we can surely abdicate it. It is our choice to make, every hour of every day.

I began to see in my circumstances a wild and open opportunity. Something beckoned—an undiscovered country for my mind and body to explore. A heady excitement blossomed, then overflowed.

After so many tears, so much confusion and despair, I realized that I had been as mindless as the leaf that helplessly clung to the tree outside my window. I had marveled at its tenacity. But after a while, it started to look a little silly. So did I, clinging to an image of a life I wanted, convincing myself that I possessed it.

It was time to release my grip, drift away, and trust that I would land on solid, nurturing ground. Nothing must end without offering a new beginning.

Winter arrived with a whisper during the night. In the morning, snow covered the mountain, the hillside, and the home where two people lived together, yet separate. The leaf had dropped from the tree, and lay restful and courageous on the soft, sparkling snow. He left that day, because I asked him to.

The memory of that time, almost a year ago now, nudges my emotions. Yes, there was sadness. But far more powerful was possibility—rich, full, and captivating. I returned to the river that I loved with renewed enthusiasm. I made more time for my friends and family, listening to their disappointments and fears, and was surprised how quickly my own melted away. I focused on problems in my community and in the world more worthy of my time than wallowing in my own drama. My path, once hazy and frightening, became clear. Passion, unbridled, took my breath away. I made my choice, and I continue to make it—every hour of every day. Now is my time to nurture the earth.

I look at the leaf, the last one of the season to move on, and thank it solemnly. Fur rubs my bare leg as the cat announces his return, the incident forgotten. I gently move him to my lap, and together we watch the woodpeckers soar past the window. My eyes are rich with joy, his with temptation. The cat returns to his chair, arches his back, and prepares for a nap. I turn back to the screen and put my hands on the keyboard. And words begin to flow. 🦃

The Last Baby

by Ruchama King

*I*t used to hurt just to say those words—the last baby. I loved being pregnant at forty-three with my fourth child. I'd enter a subway and when nobody would stand, I'd fume and glare at everybody seated, planning out scenarios of how I'd vomit or faint—but usually before I could do either someone had the decency to give me a seat. My sense of entitlement and righteous indignation felt absolutely great. When people asked me how I was feeling, I told them, in detail, of my aches and pains, dramatizing without shame, eliciting compassion from postal carriers and the dishwasher repair man and anyone within earshot. I attributed my excesses to this being the last baby.

And speaking of excess, I was huge, mountainous, a vast expanse of crater-like, uneven, ever-shifting stomach. The most I had gained in my other pregnancies was thirty-two pounds. Not this one. Here was my last hurrah, my last chance to consume as much as I wanted without guilt. Four hamburgers, five grilled-cheese sandwiches. So what? Babies need protein, 100 grams a day according to the Bradley method. I piously fulfilled my obligations. When I crossed the street at the light I was an event, a walking/waddling phenomenon. I loved the double-takes. Truck drivers, police officers, and CEOs with their Rolexes and briefcases stopped and stared. In my eighth month I thought these men fancied me. Whatever I did, wherever I went, I felt Important. And if someone dared brush too close or tried to get ahead of me in line, I gave them my Mother Brood look. Don't mess with this mama, my look said. Out of my way. I got the future inside me. I snored during this pregnancy, my gurgling upheavals so phlegmy and riotous my husband fled our queen-sized bed. I passed wind with gusto. But so what? I was pregnant, an Earth mother. Maybe in the eyes of sexy, model-beautiful magazines I was a has-been, but at forty-three I was a fertility event, a statistic-defying procreator. I was making life!

And there was my deep, dirty, dark secret. Of course I wanted a baby for its own sake. And yet—how much of being pregnant and having a baby had to do with me, me and my precious self-image, wanting to preserve my youth? I wanted to stall my "descent" into middle age, to be granted a reprieve. Fertility, pregnancy, procreation—face it, there's something exciting about a pregnant woman, a certain hum and buzz her body gives off: all that internal churning, chaotic cell multiplication, and subterranean secret life. My husband put his head to my stomach and said, "It sounds like an aquarium or an ocean in there." A pregnant woman always seemed intensely female to me, an aliveness generating more aliveness, pure youth. Passing forty, I wasn't ready to pass the baton to the younger generation. I wanted to be the younger generation. And boy, how my skin glowed right through all nine months, just like the books promised, knocking off at least five years.

This motive embarrassed me. I wanted to be pure-hearted about having a baby. My secret agenda made me feel tainted and actually filled me with pity for the embryo I was carrying inside. Poor little embriana. Your mother is using you like she would Renova. You're her Viagra-equivalent. Though it wasn't my main motive in wanting another child, it was definitely and uncomfortably there.

Was I the only older woman wanting a child for ulterior motives? Friends opened up and told me their hidden agendas. One wanted to forestall having to go back to work full time. Another friend spoke about the loneliness. She wanted a child for company in her forties and fifties. Someone else said she didn't feel she had to justify her life to herself or others if she had another child. No one would fault her if she didn't finish her doctorate. One woman wanted to outdo her sister-in-law. Someone else wanted to camouflage the fact that she couldn't lose weight. No one would blame her after the birth of a child.

My husband and I had gone back and forth for a long time, trying to decide about another child. We both had come from a family of four children, and we wanted to usher in another life to complete our family. This was more a decision that came from the head than the heart. Our other children were clamoring for another sibling. And yet my body wasn't aching and yearning to hold a little infant. I did not have baby hunger, which seemed to indicate that I wasn't ready or very interested. So we stalled for years. Our heads said, "Yes, another baby," but our bodies—my body—said no to varicose veins, no to snoring, no to back labor, no to syncopated sleep so insane I'd be denied REM states. And as long as we're at it, no to baby paraphernalia cluttering the house, no to interference with promoting my first novel, which was due the coming year, no to camping and hiking—not that we ever did that stuff, but we'd been planning on it, right?

Decision-making is enormously complex for me. In the word "decision" lies the word "incision." Any choice you make involves a cutting-off of other possibilities. In the end, what pushed me over the edge into action? The zeal for youth, that desire to be associated with vigor and life, in my mind's eye and in the eyes of others.

After one miscarriage, I got pregnant fairly easily. It was a hard ten months followed by a hard labor, which I entered into with all my being. And then Alexandra was here. What a shock. I never dreamed I'd turn into a mush ball over my last child. Those rolling fat thighs and the crazy way she rubs the sides of her head in a fury when she's tired. Cynical and analytical, I've never been a gusher. And I never knew I had so much gush inside me. I project many adult qualities onto her: patience, forgiveness (for our flaky parenting), sensitivity, social awareness. She sighs in her sleep so sweetly my husband and I give each other shocked, amazed looks: Was it this sweet with the others? Could it have been and we just hadn't noticed? I still don't know the truth—whether it's because she's the last baby or she just happens to be extraordinary.

I relish this time with her, knowing she's the last. Being a little more financially secure allows me to get the extra help I need and be less anxious. My kids treat her like candy, constantly fighting over her, wanting to hold, play with, and poke her. They bring me wipes and diapers and sing her songs and dangle silly contraptions in front of her eyes. My husband is so grateful for this awesome work of art we've produced, with God's help, he thanks me weekly for having carried and delivered this child. And then with a slight nudge he says, "Aren't you glad we pushed for this?"

Not only am I glad we pushed, but I am grateful for my shallow, ulterior motives. If not for them, I'd probably be wallowing in the hinterlands of not-pregnant-but-vaguely-wanting-to-be for years. My desire to seem young to myself and others—well, it pushed me over to the valley of decision. But you know what surprises me? How a decision reached with such ambivalence and less than noble (crass?) motives can yield pure joy. This knowledge actually comforts me in all areas of my life. It used to hurt to say those words "the last baby, the last pregnancy." Just a few weeks ago, when she was five months old, my baby learned to sit up and how happy and proud I was. Yet a part of me mourned the loss of her infancy, her total helplessness, life-filled lump that she'd been. There was no going back. Next thing she'll be eating food, and pulling herself up by the crib bars. She's going forward, filling out the dimensions of her life. I'd be fearful and miserable if she didn't progress, and yet my sadness is real.

She makes me realize I can't rely on anything to stay the same. I can't even rely on my old formulas for happiness. I must change along with her. Now I'm adjusting to the change of no more birthing. I'm going forward in my life, in a different way. If I were to be a birther forever, how awful and imprisoning that would be. I have reached a milestone, the post-birthing one, and I feel as though I'm sailing to my core, getting closer and closer to the Me I always aspired to be. But that's another story. There's a word in French that I've never encountered in English: *chantpleur*—when someone cries and sings at the same time. To hold joy and pain at the same time is an exquisite art. It reminds me of the Jewish custom of breaking a glass under the wedding canopy. Don't deny one state for the sake of the other. Experience both, and you have a shot at ecstasy.

I think I'm going to invite over all my friends who have just reached this postbirthing state. I'll call it a *chantpleur* party. We'll give away those boxes of baby clothes. We'll burn our maternity bras, and open a high-end catalogue and buy new flimsy ones. We'll toast our stretch marks, battle scars where our children are medals of honor. We'll drink wine and not worry about embryo malformation. We'll cry. After all, our lives felt so justified and complete when we were making life. We'll plan for the new life percolating inside us, crying—no, singing for creative expression. We'll mourn and we'll celebrate. We'll cry. And we'll sing. 🖎

Follow Your Passion,
Follow Your Heart

by Rebecca Hulem

I found the following powerful saying in a small book
called *The Key to Life*. Now that I am in the middle of
my life, I refer to this saying whenever I'm faced with difficult
decisions or changes that appear to be thrust upon me without
my consent.

Reflect on what has come before
Anticipate that there will be a future
Accept every present moment
You have found the key to what we call time

Reflecting back on the first half of my life, I find myself
amazed that I not only survived, but actually thrived through
much adversity. . . .

Like millions of other unfortunate people, I was born into a
family in which both parents were alcoholics. By the time I
was twelve my parents were divorced, my father was granted
custody of my two sisters and me, and the four of us moved

3,000 miles away from the only home I had ever known. Even though it appeared that I was making friends easily and adjusting to my new environment, I was riddled with self-doubt and low self-esteem.

I married young, at the age of nineteen. When I reached my twenty-third birthday I was already the mother of two beautiful children. Two children, I must add, who were born one year and three days apart. Then, six weeks after my second child was born, my husband announced that he wanted out of the marriage. So there I was, a mother of two small children— no husband and no education past high school.

I cried frequently for months after our separation, partly from anger and frustration at being in this situation, but mostly out of fear and loneliness. There were many nights I fell asleep with my clothes on and my two babies clutched in my arms.

Not long after my husband and I were separated, I received a phone call that no daughter would ever want. My mother had been murdered at the hands of a crazy person.

The resilience of the human spirit to transcend against all odds and any adverse condition has always intrigued me. Why are some people blessed with the tenacity to always make lemonade out of lemons, while others—no matter what they try—never make it?

• • •

I consider myself one of the lucky ones, a soul who has been truly blessed. For when I finally stopped crying, and with the guidance of many friends and sometimes strangers, I went on to create a good life for my children and myself.

Through the financial help of the social welfare system and student loans, I went to nursing school and received my degree as a registered nurse. I then spent the next twenty-seven years working as a registered nurse, nurse practitioner, and nurse midwife specializing in women's health. During the last twelve years of my nursing career as a nurse midwife, I delivered more than 2,000 babies and shared many valuable moments with women in all stages of their lives. But just when I thought I was at the top of my game and the hard knocks were over, I hit menopause. . . .

• • •

Menopause has been defined as the end of menstruation and the end of our childbearing years. But any woman who has experienced menopause knows that there is more to this definition than "no more periods or babies." For many women, the symptoms alone are overwhelming. Seemingly out of the blue, I had hot flashes and night sweats. I also suffered from migraine headaches, sleep disturbances, mood swings, anxiety, and fuzzy thinking. I no longer had the energy for the simplest tasks. And judging from my research and experiences caring for women in menopause, I got off easy. When I started taking my bad moods out on my family and patients, I knew I needed help.

While finding help for myself, I became passionately involved in finding help for other women, too. What evolved from my research and study came as a complete surprise to me. I discovered a passion for teaching that I must have buried long ago. And out of this passion a whole new career path appeared.

With much thought and prodding from my husband, last January (of 2003) I walked away from a well-paying, twenty-seven-year career in women's health, ventured out of the cozy corporate world and started my own company. I am now taking my love for speaking and strong desire to educate women on their many choices about menopause on the road, traveling across the United States and Canada, giving seminars to women in midlife.

I recently published my first book, called *Feeling Hot? A Humorous, Informative and Truthful Look at Menopause.* Prior to writing this book I had never written anything longer than a letter.

So why did I walk away from a very successful career in the middle of my life to start all over again? Because I have a real yearning in my heart to make a difference in women's lives. I knew I could have continued in my career as a nurse midwife. And in doing so, I would have shared many valuable experiences with women. But not knowing how much time I have left in this world, a sense of urgency came over me. A voice said: "Do it now!"

One thing I have learned in all my life experiences is that time is precious, and each of us has been put in charge of how we choose to spend our time.

Menopause and midlife bring so many physical and emotional changes that sometimes it is difficult to hear that little voice telling you what your next step should be. But once the physical symptoms start to abate and you regain your emotional balance, that still, small voice will be there, leading you forward.

Menopause is not the end; it's the beginning of a whole new second half of life. For me so far, this is the best half, and it just keeps getting better. So go ahead. . . .

Reflect on what has come before, anticipate that there will be a future, and accept every present moment. You have found the key to what we call time. ❧

The Figurine

by Linda Hepler

I opened the small package, wrapped in glossy red foil and festooned with a curly ribbon. Nestled in the crinkly tissue was a small bisque figurine, a nurse. She was dressed in a blue scrub suit and her hair was neatly lifted from her slender neck and fashioned into a bun. Her latex-gloved hands were frozen in the act of drawing serum from a vial into a syringe, presumably readying her to administer an injection. I stared at her in dismay.

Meeting my husband's expectant eyes, I stammered my thanks. "It's you," he said, proudly relating his efforts to find a meaningful Christmas gift for me. He had brought my photograph to the store where they had scanned it into a computer to create my image on the statuette. It had taken several tries to produce my likeness to his satisfaction.

But she is *not* like me, I protested silently. I have been a nurse for thirty years now, and I do not want to be a nurse any longer.

My motivation for entering nursing school was the "higher calling" that Florence Nightingale is said to have answered in the nineteenth century, the desire to help others. I had grown up poring over my mother's nursing textbooks, listening enthralled to her tales of working as an emergency room nurse. As she talked, I could see the harsh overhead lights and hear the staccato voice of the doctor barking out orders—"Scalpel!" "Sutures!"—and the clink of silver instruments against trays as the medical team worked to patch up the steady parade of patients entering the double doors. In our city, there were many who tried to solve their problems with alcohol and weapons, so there was never a dull moment. I heard about knifings and gunshot wounds and the alcoholic who had gotten into a fistfight at the local bar. Amidst this chaos and confusion, my mother was able to reach out to those in pain and anxiety and comfort them. She did not have to tell me this, though. I heard it in hushed snippets of conversation at the local grocery store, as I stood hidden behind her while she talked to a neighbor. He was thanking her for taking care of his wife when she had come to the emergency room with a heart attack. My mother looked embarrassed to hear the man's compliments, but I felt a flush of pride for her.

I wanted to be like my mother. I wanted to hear words of praise, to know that I had helped someone who needed me. I envisioned myself in a starched white uniform, stethoscope draped casually around my neck, ministering to the sick and injured, speaking the secret language of the medically initiated.

But nursing was not as I had imagined. It was simple enough for me to acclimate to the sights, sounds, and smells of the hospital, to dress an oozing leg ulcer with the acrid odor of decaying flesh assaulting my nostrils, and my patient crying out. I learned to disassociate the wound from the person, to chew gum with an open mouth, allowing the minty tang to waft upward and obliterate the stench.

It was far harder, though, to cope with the emotional toll of working with people in physical or psychic pain—or both— every day, for weeks and months and then years. In nursing school I was taught to distance myself, to keep shock, surprise, and sadness from registering on my face. I was told that I could not be "therapeutic" if I related to my patients in an emotional way. While I was able over time to train my face to remain passive, I could not instruct my heart likewise. I was horrified at the sight of a man who had failed in his suicide attempt, his gruesome monster-mask hardly recognizable as a face. I was heartbroken for the mother of a child dying of leukemia, thinking of my own healthy youngster at home. It seemed that life's collective tragedy was here, miserably huddled in this place where I spent most of my time. It shrouded me in its gray fog until I felt as if I couldn't draw air.

I began to wonder if I had made a mistake in choosing this career. I paid close attention to the other nurses to see if they felt as I did, but somehow they seemed more able to separate themselves from the pain around them. They seemed exhilarated by the work, able to feel as if they made a difference. Maybe if I tried harder I could feel the same way.

One day I was assigned a young patient who had come from surgery. Still groggy, he told me that he just learned that he had cancer. He had first noticed his left eye protruding slightly a year ago. His physician had ordered a lab test to determine if he had a thyroid problem. When the test was negative, he was reassured. It was recommended that he return if the condition worsened. A year later, the eye was bulging ominously and the man went to an ophthalmologist, then for a CAT scan, and finally to the operating room, where the cancer was discovered. He would need surgery to remove the tumor;

perhaps it had already spread to other areas. The man was crying while telling me this. He said he was scared for himself but more fearful of what would happen to his family if he died. "I have three children," he said. He begged me not to say anything to his wife until he had a chance to explain the situation to her. "I know I can help her not to be afraid."

That afternoon, I departed the hospital, leaving my child at her babysitter's house. I sat in my dark apartment and cried for my patient, for those who loved him, and for all the misery in the world. I telephoned my mother that evening to tell her about my patient and ask her how she had managed to survive nursing for all of these years. After a brief pause she said, "Oh, honey, when I became a nurse, I finally found something I did well. I love it because I'm good at it."

And she was right. Her words brought me immediately back to my childhood. My mother was not enamored of domestic life. She was a terrible cook, an often-impatient mother. But when we children were sick, it was a different story. We could be ensconced into "the big bed," thus named because my parents' bed was the largest one in the house. The record player was in this room, and my mother brought in a metal tray upon which she placed Kleenex and medications—and always a flower in a little bud vase. She would check our temperatures, serve our meals, and sponge our hot faces tenderly while Elvis Presley's voice filled the air. I felt loved and totally happy then.

But I could not feel as my mother did. I knew I was a good nurse, but being good at my job did not mean that I was helping my patients in the way I had envisioned so long ago. Helping meant more to me than attending to physical needs. Helping meant offering a backrub or spiritual comfort if it was desired. Helping meant lingering by the bedside of an old man who had pulled out his intravenous tube, demanding to go home right now. He was eighty years old, and if he only had a little bit of time left on earth, he wanted it to be spent with his wife, in his own house, with his own familiar things around him. To feel the softness of his dog's silky coat under his fingers. But I was too busy for that. Too busy administering medications, checking dressings, telephoning physicians to clarify orders, writing endless progress notes to listen to him or to others like him. I could not be the kind of nurse I want to be, so I left hospital floor nursing.

For the next ten years, I worked as an administrator of health services in a residential arts school. My patients were rich and spoiled teens who often feigned illness to escape class. For a long time, I enjoyed the challenge of being in charge, even though it meant long hours and numerous calls at home from my staff, needing guidance. I loved the artistic environment, hearing strains of Mozart and Bach as I worked. But this did not feel like nursing to me. And I did not feel totally happy with what I was doing. I considered another career direction, but at almost fifty years old, I felt as if it was too late to start over. I felt exhausted just thinking of it and resigned myself to the fact that I would never find the right career.

One summer morning on my way to a meeting, I passed a practice studio and stopped to watch a young Asian girl playing her cello. I knew her because she had come to the health office a few weeks ago, complaining of headaches and fatigue. She had told me that she was homesick for her country and I knew that this was a more likely source of her physical complaints than illness. I had seen her several times since, walking across campus, eating in the cafeteria—continuing to look listless and lethargic. But the girl in front of me now was transformed. Her beautiful face was animated, her bowing arm moving deftly across the strings of the cello, her body swaying rhythmically to the music. Observing her, I realized that her energy stemmed not from youth but from passion for her art. I continued on to my meeting, newly determined to find my own passion.

I continue to work as a nurse today, but I put in fewer hours. Much of the time I am writing, something I have always considered a hobby but never thought of as a career. It is my passion, though, and this—as well as time and determination— will help me to develop it into more than a leisure pursuit.

The nurse figurine stands on my desk, her arm broken off. Exiting the crowded elevator on my way to work after Christmas, I was jostled against the concrete wall. The figurine fell with a clatter onto the hard tile floor, the sound echoing loudly in the hallway. She glares at me reproachfully with her big green eyes, as if to say, "fix me." But I have not done so yet. I think I will wait until I am a successful writer. Then I will carefully glue the pieces together and give her to the brown-haired nursing student filled with dreams of her own. 🔖

Laughing My Way Through
the Middle "Rages"

by Dee Adams

I've never really worried about "getting older." I've always accepted whatever stage of life I happened to be experiencing. I don't remember entering my thirties with any kind of fanfare, maybe because I was busy with three kids and a divorce right about then. By the time I hit forty, I was divorced a second time, my three children were living with their father in Michigan, and I was on the road selling insurance, of all things! I do remember celebrating my fortieth birthday somewhere in Illinois, with my sister and another female sales rep.

I guess the ten years between forty and fifty were the longest and darkest of my entire life. At the time, I didn't think it had anything to do with my age, but now I believe it had *everything* to do with it. Good old "hindsight." *Now* I understand the confusion, the indecisiveness, the depression, the weight gain, and the hot flashes! There were a lot of things happening to me during those ten years, but I had no idea it was menopause.

I was working in Florida when my periods stopped at forty-one and the hot flashes started, but the available information at that time was very skimpy, so I chose to ignore the big picture—early menopause. When I was laid off from my job as marketing director and started a home business with a friend, it never entered my mind that my lack of concentration and low energy level might be due to the "change" my body was going through.

By forty-three, I had moved back to Michigan and taken a traveling sales job. *Note: Illinois at forty, Florida from forty-one to forty-two. Michigan at forty-three . . . Do you notice a pattern here?* I noticed that I couldn't see very well in the evenings as I drove from town to town, so I quit the traveling job for a part-time job that was only for the Christmas season. Big mistake. By the time I found out what was wrong, I had no job, no insurance, and no place to live. In desperation, I moved into a friend's basement and applied for Medicaid so I could get the cataract surgery I needed.

Within a month, I moved to Illinois again to be with my sister. Soon I was back to traveling, covering three states, sometimes four, still not aware that the feelings of detachment and no real focus could have anything to do with reaching middle age. By my forty-fourth birthday I had moved once again, this time to my hometown in Missouri, the only place I had any roots at all, yet I hadn't been there since I was eighteen. How many lifetimes had I lived during those years away? Seemed like several, but I finally felt I was home again.

Unfortunately, my newfound sense of security was short lived. I broke my ankle while fishing (on a day off), and things started going downhill fast. I lost my job, my insurance, and my car. I spent a full year recovering from the surgery on my ankle and trying to figure out what I was supposed to be learning from all the roadblocks that had been put in my path. This was my landing point after nearly forty-five years of no goals, no dreams, no plan of action. All I'd been doing was reacting to life, never making my life happen.

You know how they say you must "hit bottom" before you can start climbing back up? Well, that's what happened to me. In the darkest period of my life . . . clinically depressed, on welfare, alone, and seeing a psychiatrist every other week, I got the idea for a cartoon character—Minnie Pauz—that would help other middle-aged women see the lighter side of getting older. Through the process of developing this new idea (truly a miracle since I had never drawn a cartoon in my life!), I began to understand much of what I had been going through for many years. I also realized that I had always found the most joy in making others laugh.

It's taken close to eight years to learn how to draw and to reach the marketplace with my character, but I'm finally able to say that I have a focus in life as well as the confidence and the courage to make it work! I'm able to not only make a living doing something that I consider *fun,* but I'm also able to share what I've learned about life with other women who may be struggling to understand what "the change" really means. ❧

Visit Dee Adams' Web site, *www.minniepauz.com,* a popular e-zine catering to midlife women.

The Glass as Half Full

by Barbara Stephens

*T*he first time I became aware that I might be going through menopause was when I missed my monthly cycle for the very first time since the age of nine. At nine, everything that was supposed to happen to me in the usual progression of puberty was backward, such as obtaining a waistline and bouncy, glorious breasts, followed by the coveted and, much later, dreaded period. I looked exactly like any nine-year-old should look: messy hair and skinny legs that boasted a few well-earned bruises. When I discovered that my period had arrived, my mother cried for two days while I beamed with pride and called my friends to announce the good news.

It was almost a year before my body began to change. My voice lowered a bit and I was the proud and joyful owner of a bra, size 32B. It wasn't a perfect fit, but back then most bras could hold their own, even when empty. I was stared at by every boy in my sixth-grade class, winked at by seventh-grade boys whom I didn't know, and had lots of "best" friends. I enjoyed my reign as puberty queen that year and shocked everyone when I wore the first pair of fishnet hose to school. My royal status rose to impressive heights.

When I began to experience menopause at the age of thirty-eight, I didn't mourn the "end of my youth" but felt celebratory instead. I had longingly thought of the day when I could finally be free of painful cramps, bloating, tender breasts, irritability, and chocolate cravings. I had always looked upon menopause as the freeing of my spirit, and—unlike many other women—I welcomed the change with open arms.

Over the next four years, I endured every symptom the change of life had to offer. I gained weight, couldn't sleep, became insanely temperamental, and did a nightly strip show for whomever happened to be in the room at the time. I obsessed about both my daughters staying out too late at night, and even though their boyfriends were respectable, well-mannered guys who didn't drink, smoke, or go to clubs, I felt like a Samurai warrior every time they came around me. I became ridiculously cheerful when it was time for one of them to go home. Their weepy eyes would light up with a trace of hope that I might turn out to be a really nice person, after all. Indeed.

Having always enjoyed an extremely close relationship with my two daughters and son, I found myself suddenly thrust in the back seat, much like the empty water bottles, Kleenex, broken CD cases, and scattered Tic Tacs that covered the floor. I decided it was time to stop trying to fix something that obviously wasn't broken. I needed to discover myself once more and embrace my new outlook on life. I had taught my children that bravery and strength build character and self-esteem, and I knew it was time to take my own advice.

The first thing I did was to reconnect myself to my husband, a man who has shown immeasurable depth in his love for me, quietly giving his strength and friendship selflessly throughout our twenty-five-year marriage. Somehow I had pushed him to the back of the line, and it was time to bring him up front. I had been a good wife to him, still as much in love with him as the day we were married, yet at the same time I knew that I had given more of myself as a mother than as a wife.

Hell-bent on achieving the Mother of the Millennium award, I had filled the children's days with art, literature, chewy brownies, and soft cozy pajamas. At least once a week we went on an archaeological dig in the back yard to search for dinosaur bones. They cooked sausages in their tree house, sculpted figures from clay, swam in the pool, and jumped on the trampoline. One of their best memories was the time I brought them cold, red grapes to eat outside on a summer night in July. I had loved them with the best of my heart. It was time to love myself and my husband with the best of my soul.

One of the first things I did was to thoroughly educate myself about menopause, and I racked up the hours on my computer. I realized women should never view menopause as the ending of something vital in their lives, but rather the beginning of a new phase to their womanhood. With this new phase comes a deep, inner strength that can only be experienced after going through such a change, and with that strength comes a sense of self-worth, self-respect, and self-satisfaction. The more research I did, the more power I gained.

I began to love my body in a way I hadn't before, and I saw my reflection with fresh, open eyes. As I stood in front of the mirror, I saw a forty-six-year-old woman who had accumulated lines from laughter and lines from birth. Never again would I look in the mirror and see lines from worry or scars from birth.

I saw them as my badges of honor, and they told my story, my triumphs, and my accomplishments. They were etched there forever, each one a memory of days gone by, a gift that my body gave to me. They are the essence of remembrance, and a reminder of who I was, who I am, and who I will become.

When a woman is happy with herself, it shows in every single thing she does. From the clothes she wears, to how she works, or cooks, or shops, to the conversations she has with her family, it shows. I have always had a positive outlook, always seen my glass as half full, and even in the absolute worst of times I could find something to grasp on to, to give hope that the next day would be better. I tapped into that strength, which brought a whole new way of looking at menopause, my life during it, and my future without it. I was a survivor in the deepest sense, and it was time to fly my flag and, in my own way, come home.

During this time, I was approached by a friend who needed help on a summer project. Having always been a self-taught hair stylist, I had given many haircuts over the years to my friends and family. My friend was a makeup artist and needed someone to help out with hair maintenance on a project for the Discovery Channel. I had never done anything even remotely like this, and after a little coaxing from my husband, I decided to give it a try. The project was a success, and upon completion I was offered the position of hairstylist and makeup artist for a future project that would involve several episodes for a series. The project wasn't to begin for four weeks, which gave me time to put together my own customized makeup kit and to brush up on the latest techniques.

My husband was incredibly helpful during this time, and we had many conversations about my new job. Being an artist by nature, he had much to offer and many helpful suggestions. By profession, he is a prosthetist and anaplastologist, and I gained a renewed level of respect for the depth of his knowledge, patience, and guidance.

To my surprise, I discovered I was a natural at skin-tone matching. I spent time on my computer researching different lines of makeup, studying the colors and versatility of makeup. During my research, I became interested in corrective and camouflage makeup. Upon further study of the subject, I realized I was a perfect candidate for training because the basis of this type of makeup is skin-tone matching. I obtained a few samples from Linda Seidel Natural Cover Makeup, a makeup company based in Maryland, and after trying them I decided on this line for my personalized makeup kit.

I was very impressed with Seidel's makeup and how it could be used to help with scars, birthmarks, and various skin disorders, and I told everyone about it. I received an e-mail from a gentleman in France inquiring about her line of makeup, and he eventually purchased a kit from her company. This got the attention of Linda Seidel and I received a phone call from her assistant. They frequently held training seminars on the East Coast, but had never come as far south as Virginia. They were willing to come to my hometown of Virginia Beach to hold the next one, and I was to be their hostess and guest. I received full training from Linda herself and obtained a certification in corrective and camouflage makeup. I soon discovered that Linda had been in several major fashion magazines, had received numerous prestigious awards for her work and dedication, and was featured in *People Magazine* and *Ripley's Believe It or Not.*

Over the next four years, I obtained work from CBS, The Learning Channel, the Discovery Channel, MTV, VH-1, PAX

TV, American Movie Classics, and NASA. My work was submitted for an Emmy, and even though I didn't receive one, I am incredibly proud to have been considered.

Menopause brought to me many wonderful and exciting experiences, and I discovered myself along the way. My husband and I drew closer together during this time, bringing our friendship and love for one another to a new level of intimacy, one that we still share today. I have come full circle, and I am a better woman because of menopause. It enriched my life and gave new dimension to all that I have. It wasn't just the change of life; it was My Change of Life. Making it personal made it rewarding, unique, and individual. I have loved every single minute of it. Well, *almost* every single minute. I could have done without those hot flashes; however, I think my husband would disagree. They taught me how to strip, something he greatly enjoys to this day. See⸮ I told you my glass is always half full. ❧

A Resurrection of the Body

by Mary Jacobs

Sweating and pedaling up a hill in Vermont, my cycling companions and I began to bemoan the inevitable soreness we'd face the next day. We were all middle-aged, and we were all on vacation, exerting ourselves more than usual. We knew we were going to pay.

"You know," one of my friends joked, "when I was young, I'd see those old people with all these aches and pains, and I thought, "I'm never gonna do that."

Ah, didn't we all? Didn't we all make such naive vows, about how we'd stay slim and healthy and somehow will ourselves immune to the indignities of aging? And didn't our bodies, eventually, betray us? Maybe just in little ways—an age spot here, a wrinkle there, a few sore muscles after a bike ride that wouldn't have fazed our younger selves. Or maybe with big betrayals—disease, disability.

And yet, I learned, even again, battle-weary bodies can perform small miracles. I'll never pass for a twenty-five-year-old, but I can appreciate my forty-three-year-old body's strength and wisdom in ways I never did before.

My story starts with my body's biggest betrayal—cancer. When I was thirty-four, I was diagnosed with Hodgkins lymphoma. That first bout in 1994 wasn't so bad; I weathered chemo and radiation sporting colorful hats and fun wigs. And I was confident because Hodgkins is the "good" cancer, a highly curable kind.

But in 1997, when the Hodgkins recurred, I entered that no man's land of gut-gnawing uncertainty. This time I felt divorced from my body, utterly betrayed. "Body," I said, "you've really blown it this time."

Even though we weren't on speaking terms, my body managed to survive with stoic grace, "sailed" through treatment, as my doctor put it. It didn't feel like sailing, but I had no problems other than the expected nausea and fatigue. After twenty-three days in the hospital for a stem cell transplant (a type of bone marrow transplant), I was so weak I could barely walk the few feet from the car to my front door.

Gradually, I began to recover, but my energy level remained low. Having exercised regularly before, I knew I'd have more energy if I exercised a little. But I viewed my body as gimpy and flawed. Better not push it. I slept instead.

As fate would have it, in early 1998, my crafty editor asked me to interview cyclist Lance Armstrong for a newspaper story. After a fierce battle with testicular cancer, Lance had just returned to competitive cycling.

I asked him, "Do you ever worry that by pushing yourself so hard physically you might bring back the cancer?"

"If my doctors told me to get off the bike, I'd get off the bike," he told me. "But as long as they tell me that it's okay, I'm going to compete."

His words resonated for me. I realized: I couldn't get another body. I could only make decisions with the best information available. Lance had had cancer, but that didn't mean his body was gimpy or flawed. (In fact, the guy is borderline superhuman.) The cancer just happened. It was time for me to get back on the bike, too.

So I went back to the health club. I took it very, very gradually, but I kept on. Meanwhile, Lance went on to win the Tour de France—and then repeated himself several times over, becoming a five-time winner. I still shake my head in amazement. If Lance can overcome cancer and win the Tour de France, I thought, at least I can get in shape.

At the beginning of 2001, I came across an article about the Danskin Women's Triathlon in Austin, Texas. Even before cancer, this would have been a daunting challenge. It was just the thing.

I checked with my oncologist first. "Go for it," he told me. An avid bicyclist, he even offered me a few training tips.

The next day I told a group of girlfriends I was going to run a triathlon.

"You're nuts," they said. But a week later, they all signed up.

So we began training together. We spent mornings biking around the local lake, sweating and puffing. We swam lap after lap and ran mile after mile. Since we all had children in the same school, we nicknamed ourselves "the Significant Mothers" (slogan: "Somebody's gonna get hurt").

At times I got discouraged. I was slower than everybody. I worked hard, and I improved, but I never caught up. One day, biking along at the back of the pack, I passed a man sitting in his car smoking a cigarette. "I'm ahead of him," I thought. "Way ahead!"

In June, we traveled together to Austin for the triathlon. My family came along to cheer me on, including my nine-year-old daughter, who I like to think was paying attention. I bought her a T-shirt that read: "My Mom Tri's."

The first "wave" of participants, the expert class, dashed into the lake to start the race, stroking furiously as a swarm of angry bees. Next was my wave, a group of about twenty-five cancer survivors. We looked more like a flotilla. We paddled along, chatting. We were, literally, just glad to be there.

After the half-mile swim, I hopped on my bike for a thirteen-mile ride—full of hills—followed by an agonizing three-mile run/stagger.

I wasn't fast, but I finished. (And I must tell you, I did beat a few twenty-five-year-olds.) At the finish line, someone handed me a medal inscribed with these words: "The woman who starts the race is not the same woman who finishes the race."

I know I wasn't. My oncologists had given me back my health, but the triathlon gave me back my body.

I realized I owed my body a big apology. I thought of the day I had returned from the hospital, chemo-weary and barely able to walk. Yes, I had taken care of myself: eating, training, resting. But my body, with its awesome, invisible wisdom, did the real work. It handled an onslaught of disease and chemo and put itself back together again—then ran its first triathlon at the age of forty-one.

"Body," I said, "you're all right." ❧

The Old in One Another's Arms

by Davida Rosenblum

alph, my brilliant, adored, iconoclastic, charismatic filmmaker husband of forty-seven years, died suddenly in the fall of 1995. A little more than two months later, I learned that the wife of my very first lover, whom I hadn't seen in almost half a century, had passed away at the same time. I was stunned by the double coincidence: Marc and I married our respective mates within a month of each other, and we had become widowed two weeks apart.

Marc was not only my first lover; he was also my first love. For nearly two years we'd "dated," a word that in those days could mean anything from a weekly movie to "sleeping together," another euphemism of the late 1940s. Besides a commonality of interests, we shared a hearty appetite for sex, though we were novices at the time. Ultimately, Marc chose to marry Kitty, his English sweetheart whom he'd met during World War II, but his image remained with me over the entire course of a difficult but richly textured marriage. Though in his last years Ralph had almost mellowed into the mate I'd always wanted, he was not Marc—or at least not the Marc deified by memory into the model of a lover no mere mortal could match.

Overwhelmed by conflicting emotions, I spent the next several hours agonizing over the news. Finally, I sent him a brief condolence note: "My deepest sympathy on your recent loss. Having just suffered a similar loss myself, I know what you must be feeling." It ended with a three-word sign-off, the exact configuration of which eluded me for the better part of an hour. I chose, finally, "With remembered affection."

Marc's reply arrived three days later. I opened it with a pounding heart. Inside were thanks for having written, and an invitation to call if I shared his view that meeting again might be "therapeutic at worst, entrancing at best." And call I did, after a long afternoon of staring at the phone, wondering what I would say. After some awkward conversation punctuated with long silences—how does one gracefully span fifty years in one phone conversation?—Marc suggested meeting for dinner.

"Why don't you come here?" I proposed. We made a date for the following night. Never were thirty hours so suffused with a combination of dread and eagerness.

The doorbell rang at precisely 6:30. I took a deep breath and opened the door. There, bearing a bottle of wine, a bouquet of tulips, and an expression as tragic as the one I'd been seeing in the mirror since the death of my husband, was an almost unrecognizable Marc. He looked older than the seventy-two years I figured him to be. His jawline was nearly obliterated by the dewlaps that age invariably brings, and there was a swath of bare scalp where wiry reddish hair had once grown. My young lover was nowhere to be seen. We stood staring at each other for some time; I suppose he was looking at me with similar thoughts.

We spent the next four hours weeping over our losses and describing our lives during the intervening years, all the while picking with little interest at the lavish spread I had prepared.

As we said goodbye, Marc put an arm around my shoulder and gave me what started as the barest of hugs—only to become a full body hug that lasted for an astonishing several minutes. As it ended, he kissed me lightly. There was a faint suggestion of tongue. Hesitantly, I met his with the tip of my own.

"Oh, God!" I thought despairingly, "here we go again."

Marc phoned two days later. "I owe you a dinner," he said, without preamble. "What are you doing this afternoon?"

We decided on a movie. I suppose we weren't sure we had anything more to say to each other. We both arrived at the theater a full half-hour early. As we talked, I gradually became aware that his depression was gone. He was cheerful, lively, and amusing.

"What on earth happened between Monday and now?" I asked, unable to hide my astonishment. "You're so different!"

"It was the hug," he said.

We took our seats just as the lights dimmed. Within minutes, a creeping anxiety overtook me and blotted out whatever was taking place on the screen. During our conversation, everything about Marc that I had once found irresistible was again manifest. I knew that some landmark events would soon be taking place, chief among them a trip to the bedroom. And I had a problem with that.

I, too, had changed. My body now bore all the stigmata of fifty years of aging—stretch marks from two pregnancies and a hysterectomy scar the least of them. With a sinking heart, I did a quick inventory of every defect, sure that they would be an immediate turn-off for anyone who hadn't experienced their accretion gradually over the years.

When I finished contemplating my own shortcomings, I tried to visualize Marc's. The prospect of dealing with a body that might be in comparable shape, even if I had known it intimately half a century before, was less than beguiling. Besides, it occurred to me that he might no longer be sexually viable—my impression was that most men in their seventies weren't. And, even though at our age it probably wouldn't matter one way or another, the process of discovery was unimaginable.

As we walked toward Sixth Avenue looking for a place to eat, Marc mentioned that he'd become a bird-watcher since his retirement, and asked if I'd like to accompany him to his favorite wildlife preserve that Saturday. By now I was crazed. Here was Marc laying himself out for me like a picnic lunch, and all I could think of was the dreaded moment when we would find ourselves in bed. Between bouts of panic and the need to keep up my end of the conversation, I considered the possibilities. On the one hand, he might run screaming from the room. On the other hand, *I* might not be moved to do anything more than—literally—sleep together. In light of our youthful passion, I found this scenario the most depressing of all.

As we neared the corner, I turned to face him. My next words came as a complete surprise. "You'll be staying over tonight," I said in a conversational tone. "Shall I pick up some bagels for breakfast?"

I stood there immobilized, aghast at my audacity. Marc looked at me thoughtfully for a long moment. "Bagels would be nice," he said.

Dinner was tense, at least for me—just one more intolerable delay on the way to the moment of truth. One block from my apartment, we stopped to pick up the bagels. I nearly groaned aloud when Marc expressed a preference for poppy seed. I have always hated poppy seeds. By unhappy coincidence, they'd been Ralph's favorite too.

I managed to kill five minutes by completely rearranging the closet as I hung up our coats. I killed another five moving the bagels with exaggerated care into poppy-seed-proof plastic bags. It was now seven minutes after nine. There was nothing to do but make a pot of coffee and talk some more; bedtime at 9:07 was for impatient lovers, and I was certainly not that.

Time passed in excruciating increments. I kept looking at my watch, hoping both that the hands wouldn't move and that they would move faster. Marc seemed unnaturally calm. After several centuries, midnight arrived. The next move would have to be mine, it appeared, as Marc seemed perfectly content to sit and chat all night. I stood up.

"Well," I said, in a voice more suitable to an execution than a seduction, "I guess it's time."

One of my flowered flannels was hanging on the back of the bathroom door. For a moment I considered getting under the covers in the altogether rather than putting it on, but that, I felt, would be giving myself an unnecessary handicap. Better to wear the flannel with its pink peonies and red cabbage roses and take my chances. I am by nature more flannel than silk, so my future would rest on the former. Shivering, I slid the nightgown over my head and got into bed.

"Okay," I called weakly, and placed my fate in the hands of the gods.

There will not be here a description, elliptical or otherwise, of what ensued. I am the wrong generation for that. Suffice it to say that yes—he could—and our lovemaking was as delicious, intoxicating, and graceful—yes, graceful, as it had ever been in our youth. There was not one moment of awkwardness; however altered, our bodies were merely the conduits of our mutual need and our joy in having rediscovered each other.

It has been more than a year since that momentous night. We continue to mourn our lost companions, but grief is now part of the backdrop of our new life rather than a wrenching interruption of it. Each day, however we choose to spend it, is a miracle; we are endlessly surprised by this unexpected gift and the pleasure we take in each other's company. It is all the proof we need that there is indeed life after death.

I gaze at Marc blissfully over our morning bagels—still poppy seed, I regret to say—hold on to his hand during our afternoon walks, and at night lie spoon-fashion against his large, comfortable body. He is old and so am I, but that knowledge, too, is part of the backdrop. Sometimes I think wistfully of the years I will never have with my husband—and paradoxically, those I missed spending with Marc. But mostly, I am content. The young Marc is gone forever; the dream is gone as well. But I no longer need either. The circle has been closed and, with gratitude, love, and mutual delight, we are in it together.

Recommended Web Sites

www.power-surge.com
www.minniepauz.com
www.cronechronicles.com
www.theredhatsociety.com
www.aarpmagazine.org
www.bestyears.com
www.inherprime.com
www.fifty-plus.net
www.thirdage.com
www.owl-national.org
www.gorgeousgrandma.com
www.neatwomeninc.com
www.2young2retire.com
www.seniorwomen.com
www.ourselves.com

www.hopemag.com
www.tickleyoursoul.com
www.boomercafe.com
www.50plusexpeditions.com
www.laterlife.com
www.50plus-feeling30.com
www.myprimetime.com
www.boomersint.org
www.mothersover40.com
www.wooferclub.com
www.aginghipsters.com
www.seniorwomen.com
www.womenofacertainage.com
www.beautybeyond50.com

Recommended Reading

Barbach, Lonnie. *The Pause: Positive Approaches to Perimenopause and Menopause.* New York: Plume, 1993.

Bauer-Maglin, Nan, and Radosh, Allie. *Women Confronting Retirement.* New Jersey: Rutgers University Press, 2003.

Corio, Laura E., and Kahn, Linda. *The Change Before the Change, Everything You Need to Know to Stay Healthy in the Decade Before Menopause.* New York: Bantam, Doubleday and Dell, 2000.

Dowling, Collette. *Red Hot Mamas: Coming into Our Own at Fifty.* New York: Bantam Press, 1996.

Friedan, Betty. *The Fountain of Age.* New York: Simon and Schuster, 1993.

Gittleman, Ann Louise. *Before the Change: Taking Charge of Your Perimenopause.* San Francisco: Harper, 1998.

Gittleman, Ann Louise. *Super Nutrition for Menopause: Take Control of Your Life and Enjoy New Vitality.* New York: Pocket Books, 1993.

Greer, Germaine. *The Change: Women, Aging and the Menopause.* New York: Fawcett, 1992.

Heilbrun, Carolyn G. *The Last Gift of Time: Life Beyond Sixty.* New York: Dial Press, 1997.

Hoffman, Lisa. *Better Than Ever: The 4-Week Workout Program for Women Over Forty.* New York: Contemporary, 1997.

Lee, Dr. John R. *What Your Doctor May Not Tell You About Menopause.* New York: Warner Books, 1996.

Love, Susan M. *Dr. Susan Love's Hormone Book: Making Informed Choices About Menopause.* New York: Random House, 1997.

Marston, Stephani. *If Not Now, When? Reclaiming Ourselves at Midlife.* New York: Warner Books, 2001.

Northrup, Dr. Christiane. *The Wisdom of Menopause: Creating Physical and Emotional Health and Healing During the Change.* New York: Bantam, Doubleday and Dell.

Pogrebin, Letty Cottin. *Getting over Getting Older.* Boston: Little, Brown, 1996.

Reichman, Judith. *I'm Too Young to Get Old: Health Care for Women over Forty.* New York: Random House, 1996.

Schwartz, Erika. *The Hormone Solution: Naturally Alleviate Symptoms of Hormone Imbalance from Adolescence Through Menopause.* New York: Warner Books, 2002.

Shandler, Nina. *Estrogen—the Natural Way: Over 250 Recipes Using Natural Plant Estrogens for Women.* New York: Villard Books, 1997.

Sheehy, Gail. *The Silent Passage.* New York: Picket Books, revised 1995.

Sheehy, Gail. *New Passages: Mapping Your Life Across Time.* New York: Random House, 1995.

Smith, Kathy, and Miller, Robert. *Moving Through Menopause: The Complete Program for Exercise, Nutrition and Total Wellness.* New York: Warner Books, 2002.

Warga, Claire. *Menopause and the Mind: The Complete Guide to Coping with Memory Loss, Foggy Thinking, Verbal Confusion, and Other Cognitive Effects of Perimenopause and Menopause.* New York: Simon & Schuster, 1999.

Waterhouse, Debra. *Outsmarting the Midlife Fat Cell: Winning Weight Control Strategies for Women over 35 to Stay Fit Through Menopause.* New York: Hyperion, 1999.

Weaver, Frances. *The Girls with the Grandmother Faces: A Celebration of Life's Potential for Those over 55.* New York: Hyperion, 1996